A Celtic Resurrection

A CELTIC RESURRECTION

The Diary of a Split from the Church

ROBERT VAN DE WEYER

Fount
An Imprint of HarperCollinsPublishers

Fount Paperbacks is an Imprint of
HarperCollins*Religious*
Part of HarperCollins*Publishers*
77–85 Fulham Palace Road, London W6 8JB

First published in Great Britain
in 1996 by Fount Paperbacks

1   3   5   7   9   10   8   6   4   2

Copyright © Robert Van de Weyer 1996

Robert Van de Weyer asserts the moral right to be
identified as the author of this work

A catalogue record for this book is
available from the British Library

ISBN 0 00 627984 8

Printed and bound in Great Britain by
Caledonian International Book Manufacturing Ltd, Glasgow, G64

INTRODUCTION

When the people of Upton gathered in their village hall, and decided to sever their financial and administrative links with their bishop, I knew that something of much wider interest and significance was unfolding. So I began to keep a diary of, or rather a commentary on, the events. This book is that commentary.

I didn't anticipate that within a few days the quiet lanes of that tiny English village would be packed with television crews and newspaper reporters. Nor could I have known that the decision made that evening in Upton would have a direct bearing on five parishes in the Breckland area of Norfolk, who have staged an even more highly publicized rebellion against their bishop. Upton has also had an indirect influence on a group of parishes in Suffolk, and on an ecumenical church in a run-down area of Peterborough. And, judging by the vast number of letters I have received, the whole saga is seen by many across the country and beyond as a beacon of hope.

I wrote my commentary on loose sheets of A4 paper and put them in a file. I opened the file on 3 February 1994, and marked it 'A Celtic Resurrection'. I have always been a devotee of Celtic Christianity, and I believed that what the people of Upton were doing was essentially Celtic in spirit. As the months passed, that title seemed increasingly appropriate: the parishes were receiving a breath of new life, which blew away the dark cloud of gloom which hangs over so much British Christianity and promised a bright future. So I have preserved it as the title of this book.

During the past 18 months my own thoughts and attitudes have moved rapidly forward in the Celtic direction and much of this book is concerned with how Celtic ideas and ideals can apply today. I believe that my own Celtic journey is shared not only by the people in the churches described in this book, but by people throughout Britain and beyond. This is why the media sensed that these stories have wide public interest, and it is why I offer this diary-commentary for publication.

Events in Upton, Breckland and the other churches have not reached a neat conclusion. But the churches have all set out firmly on the Celtic path, and are most unlikely to turn back. I know of many other churches who are also walking along this path, and far more churches that would like to find their way on to it. The great Celtic seers taught us not to expect conclusions to our journey; what matters, they said, is that we should travel in faith. It is to the faith of the people described in these pages that I dedicate this book.

3 February 1994

The meeting wasn't a muddle, as I had anticipated. About 20 people spoke, and all seemed very clear about the issues involved; the other 30 people nodded and shook their heads at the appropriate times. Nor was the meeting angry and defiant, as I had feared; given the enormity of what was being decided, people were remarkably calm. Most astonishing of all, it was unacrimonious. Only a fortnight ago an open meeting to discuss the catering arrangements in the village hall almost came to blows over the brand of tea to be stocked. But when it came to deciding that they no longer want a vicar, and will from henceforth manage the church themselves, the people of Upton spoke with a single voice.

Mike Newton was at his best as chairman. Normally he prides himself on being a matter-of-fact businessman, who pleads ignorance on all things 'spiritual'. But last night he dropped that guise, and showed – to his wife's visible amazement – a firm grasp of what the village must do if the people are to organize their own pastoral ministry. He began by thanking me for my work as unpaid vicar over the past 11 years. 'You served as much by what you didn't do, as by what you did,' he said, with an ironic smile, 'so since your resignation last September we've hardly noticed the difference.' Somebody chipped in with the old joke: 'Your visits to people in the village were so rare that when your car appeared outside someone's house we knew the grim reaper was near.' Mike then said that for many years I had been publicly advocating fewer clergy, both to save money and to encourage local people to 'plug the gaps'. 'So now we intend to take your advice,' he concluded.

For a brief period Mike was allowed to be a businessman again, when someone asked about the church's financial affairs. Waving an article on the subject cut out from the *Financial Times*, Mike explained how the Church of England at national level is going bust, so that the salaries of clergy would in future have to be financed by the weekly collection in local churches. And he drew a diagram on a large sheet of paper to show that a small village like Upton couldn't pay even a quarter share of a priest's salary, *and* keep its ancient church in good repair. People readily agreed that the building was more important than the clergy: 'Vicars come and go, but the church must stay forever.'

Then someone asked what vicars actually do, and whether lay people can do the same. Mike turned to me for enlightenment. I replied rather quizzically: 'The church in Upton has flourished for the past eleven years with my doing almost nothing. So whatever vicars have done in the past, you are already doing it splendidly.' The questioner suggested that my answer 'clinches it – we should write to the bishop to tell him he can keep his vicars.' Mike reworded the proposal in more formal language, and put it to the meeting. As every hand rose, a group of ladies on the back row slipped off into the kitchen, and moments later reappeared with cups of tea and large slices of cake. The only hard words I heard during the entire evening were from an elderly woman complaining that the brand of tea 'tastes like dishwater'.

This morning I went back to Upton and walked up the village street. The people I met seemed stunned at what they had done, and wondered 'if we'll get away with it'.

7 February 1994

Upton village street on a Monday morning in winter is usually very quiet. The commuters have caught the 7.14 train from Huntingdon to King's Cross, and the shoppers have taken the daily bus into Peterborough; only a handful of mums with prams, and some old people walking their dogs, venture out. But this morning three camera crews, two radio journalists and five newspaper reporters have descended on the Cambridgeshire village, all eager to hear about Upton's decision to 'opt out' of the Church of England. My naïveté is responsible for this incursion. I had made a brief reference to Upton in an article for the *Guardian*; their religious affairs editor smelt a story, and investigated further; and his article on Saturday was picked up by the rest of the pack.

The pack left us at about lunch time, and charged off to Ely to interview the diocesan authorities. This evening, on both BBC and ITV, we saw the results. The Upton people came over as cheerful and sensible. The authorities by contrast were visibly nettled; the PR officer for the diocese even suggested they might padlock Upton church to prevent the people worshipping there – and then hastily added that 'we hope this nuclear option won't prove necessary'. A few minutes ago a Press Agency reporter telephoned me, quoted a press release issued by the diocese, and asking for my comments. The press release accuses me of having persistently preached to the people of Upton 'about money, and not the gospel', and that this unchristian teaching had caused them to revolt. I could probably sue the PR officer for defamation of character – but that would certainly be going against the gospel.

I had thought that religious stories needed a sexual angle to take off. But all of us involved in Upton church are boringly heterosexual and faithful. The media interest seems to reflect deep public anxiety about the future of religion. The great majority of people, opinion polls consistently affirm, believe in God and pray

3

to him, and also regard Jesus Christ as their primary source of moral guidance. And they want their parish church to exist as a symbol of God's presence – that's why they contribute so generously to appeals to repair the roof. Yet they feel increasingly cut off from religious institutions. Bishops and clergy seem remote and detached from reality, and churchgoing is regarded as little more than a hobby for those who enjoy it. So Upton seems like a flash of light in the spiritual darkness: an entire community is taking responsibility for its church – both the building itself and the spiritual ministry which emanates from it.

I feel both excited and frightened. My reasons for resigning as unpaid vicar were in part personal: I do not enjoy being in charge of anything, and am bad at it. But my resignation was also a matter of principle. I had come firmly to the conclusion that people like me, called to be preachers and prophets, should not also be managers. Each congregation should manage its own affairs, using to the full the various gifts which God has bestowed on its members. Churches generally flourish in the gap between one vicar leaving and another arriving, when the congregation is compelled to look after itself. So why not extend the gap indefinitely? I'm also increasingly disturbed by a barrier between institutional religion and the spiritual needs of the bulk of the population; and, in ways I cannot fully describe, I sense that the clergy and the bishops are the bricks which form that barrier. When I tendered my resignation I openly said to the four churches in my charge: 'Either return to the fold and join a larger group of parishes under a full-time salaried priest or strike out on your own.' Two of my parishes decided immediately to return to the fold; one of them, Hamerton, will be meeting in a fortnight. I can still hardly believe that Upton has taken my advice with such conviction.

Apart from a brief bout of media interest, Upton's decision has only one immediate consequence: that it ceases its financial contribution to the diocese, and starts to give money directly to churches in particular need. But I know that, in ways none of us can predict, our lives will in the long-term be profoundly changed – my life, the life of the parish, and perhaps the life of parishes far away.

24 February 1994

Upton has a new village hall, heated on cold winter evenings by shining electric radiators. Hamerton's village hall was built at the turn of the century. Originally it had a huge open fire on which logs from the nearby copse were thrown. But modern village people – especially the farmers who spend all day in air-conditioned tractors – can't cope with such a messy arrangement. So about 30 years ago the fireplace was boarded up, and electric fan heaters were installed on the wall just above head height. When they are turned on the top half of one's body gets warm, while the legs and feet remain icy. Worse still, their loud whirr forces people to raise their voices. So at the end of a meeting one's throat is hoarse and one's head aches.

The hall was packed last night to discuss the future of the church. The media interest at Upton had prompted almost the entire village – about 70 people – to attend. Hamerton likes to conduct its business formally, according to strict rules of procedure. So the meeting began with a proposal from a computer consultant that the heaters be turned off. The chairman – a highly intelligent lawyer, David Way, who is also a churchwarden – asked for a seconder; a farmer's widow, in a thick woollen coat, put up her hand. David asked for any amendments to the proposal. Two elderly ladies put up their hands; so a discussion ensued, in which the differing benefits of warmth and silence were finely balanced. The oldest person in the hall, with a hint of indignation in her voice, reminded the meeting that the heaters had been given in memory of a former stalwart of the village hall committee. This seemed to swing the debate; a vote was taken, and the heaters were left on. Within a few minutes the combination of their warmth and the heat emanating from so many bodies made us all distinctly uncomfortable; but, since the vote had been duly minuted, nothing could be done.

At first, views about the future of the church seemed even more divided than feelings about the heaters. The churchgoers, both regulars and occasional, were unanimous in wanting to follow Upton's lead. But another group, made up entirely of men, had clearly decided in advance that they should uphold the established order. They proclaimed strongly the need for a full-time vicar, and they asserted that the churchgoers should raise enough money to pay for one. Not unnaturally, some of the churchgoers didn't like being told their duties by 'a bunch of agnostics', to which one of the men, a sombre character draped in an outsize gaberdine raincoat, replied that he had once sung in a church choir.

David skilfully steered the discussion away from these theological obstructions to the hard facts. He offered his estimates of the sums required over the next ten years to pay for a vicar and maintain the church fabric, and even the upholders of the established order blanched. The former chorister questioned the figures, but David had done his homework thoroughly. 'Where does Robert fit in to all this?' someone called out from the back. 'We get him free,' one of the churchgoers replied. There was a happy hum of friendly approval of my ministry; and someone even said I was 'very nice' – not a view shared any longer by bishops and archdeacons. I replied that, while I was deeply grateful for their loving support, I was actually irrelevant to the issue; what matters is whether the parish as a whole could commit itself to a shared Christian ministry.

By this time the heat had become stifling. A rather confused debate followed about the meaning of shared ministry. To my delight, the churchgoers, who already practise it in all manner of quiet and hidden ways, seemed to have a firm grasp. One quoted Paul's Epistle to the Corinthians on the subject; another said, 'We've heard Robert bang on about it often enough, so we jolly well should have got the idea'; a third added, with a wink in my direction, 'Since Robert has done so little these past years, we've been thrown in at the deep end.' But the defenders of the establishment, especially the former chorister, couldn't get the idea at all. 'A vicar's a vicar, and ever more shall be,' the chorister pronounced.

If I had been chairing the meeting, I would have risked taking a vote; I suspect the establishment group would have abstained, and everyone else voted in favour of following Upton's lead. But David, with his lawyer's caution, thanked everyone for their attendance, and said that the church council would consider the views expressed in depth before making a decision. To my surprise, everyone accepted this statement without protest; perhaps they were desperate for liquid to rehydrate their parched bodies. David read a suitable collect from the *Book of Common Prayer*, and we all dispersed.

9 March 1994

Since the burst of publicity last month I have received three sorts of letter.

The first – only a few – has been Anglican hate mail, mainly from clergy. They see me as a threat to the 'integrity' – a favourite word – of the Church of England. This integrity seems to depend on parishes sending to the central funds whatever sums are demanded, and accepting whatever clergy the bishop chooses to appoint. And in upholding such a system these clergy see themselves as defending the ancient traditions of the Church. In reply I point out that the system is actually quite modern. Until the Ecclesiastical Commissioners were formed last century, there were no central funds; and within living memory parishes still paid their clergy directly from glebe and tithe income. As for appointing clergy, this traditionally lay in the hands of local patrons; and in Saxon times, when the parish system was formed, the priests were often chosen from the local people. So in taking authority over money and ministry back to itself, Upton is actually returning to the old ways.

The second category of letter comes mainly from harassed churchwardens and treasurers, in despair at the state of church finances. They are filled with anger at the Church Commissioners – the successor to the 19th-century body – for losing a billion pounds through property speculation; and they see themselves as the victims of this folly, since contributions from parishes must make up the shortfall. They mostly point out that they are already delaying vital repairs to the church fabric in order to meet the financial demands from the central body. And they ask what would happen if, like Upton, they stop paying. The simple answer is that, apart from receiving nasty letters from their archdeacon, nothing will happen; their priest will continue to receive his monthly salary cheque. But I point out that such a policy would be dishonest, since it would put the cost of paying their vicar on to other parishes. The only fair way of reducing or eliminating their payments would be to take on some or all of the vicar's functions themselves – as Upton is doing.

The third type of letter hails Upton as the saviour of the rural church. It seems that lots of people have long since concluded that the present system is neither viable nor desirable. Some of these letters are from clergy in country parishes who see their presence as actually disabling the lay people from exercising their spiritual gifts. As one parson put it: 'While I'm here, available six days a week, people expect me to do all the jobs; but if there were no vicar, the people would soon take on my various tasks – and in most cases do them much better.' The obvious solution is for him to resign. But in a sad final paragraph he points out that 'priest-craft' is the only skill he possesses, so for his own survival he must remain in his post; he hopes that his group of rural parishes will follow Upton's example when he retires.

Strangely, I think the first category of letter is nearer the heart of the matter than the other two. Certainly finance is a terrible problem. In many places the Church of England's main activity has become fund-raising, simply to maintain itself. Indeed if I moved into a village today as an ordinary lay person I would be very cautious about attending church at all, for fear of being sucked into an endless round of jumble sales and fêtes, coffee mornings and bazaars; I wonder how many people are actually deterred from the church for this reason. And, of course, I also agree that clergy often impede the ministry of the church rather than enable it.

But these are symptoms of a more fundamental problem. The 'integrity' of the church is actually its fatal flaw. There is nothing in the gospels which suggests Jesus wanted to create large religious institutions, with great hierarchies of bishops and priests, requiring huge sums of money. On the contrary he fought against these things; he hailed the widow with her mite as his true disciple. Throughout Christian history there have been people and movements to restore the primitive simplicity of the gospel. I see the decision by Upton as a very tentative and uncertain step in that direction.

21 March 1994

The postman continues to bring large quantities of mail about Upton, almost all in support. Mostly I write short letters in reply. But one particular letter I received last week stood out: it was from a clergyman in Suffolk called Richard Titford. He said that he wondered if Upton might have some clues for the future of his ministry. I decided to telephone him and suggest we get together; and last Friday afternoon I turned up at his vicarage in the tiny village of Edwardstone.

He is a little older than I am – in his late 40s – and spent his early adult years running the family business making zip fasteners. But even at first glance it's hard to see him as anything other than a country parson. He has a deep, gentle voice with a slight stammer, a ruddy complexion and a round tummy that suggest he enjoys in moderate quantities the good things of life, and he listens intently to everything one says. I can imagine that both in a family crisis and at a summer tea party he is the ideal companion. When he speaks of his parishioners, his pleasure in their virtues and their foibles – and even in their petty squabbles – is evident. And he talks of the three church buildings in his patch with glowing pride. In addition to all this, he is highly intelligent and well-read. If all rural clergy were like him, people would happily pay the quota.

Yet Richard Titford feels increasingly burdened by his position. He loves his work, but he feels uncomfortable that his parishioners are compelled to pay a certain sum each year to the diocese for his services; and he dislikes too the sense of being employed by the diocese, rather than by the people to whom he ministers. In fact, he is objecting to the whole notion of a hierarchical church. I asked him whether he would prefer to be paid directly by his parishes, according to what they were willing and able to give. 'I hadn't thought of that,' he replied; and after a pause he added, 'it would be rather embarrassing'. He then said that he envied my position, of being free of any financial attachment to the diocese, and offering my ministry freely to the parishes. And he was wondering if he might do the same, resigning his position, yet remaining in the village, and offering to serve the parishes without charge.

We talked in detail about the various potential snags of this plan. In particular, he would have to earn his living by some other means; and apart from knowing about zip fasteners he doesn't have any skills to sell. And even if he could solve the financial problem, his parishioners would need to commit themselves to taking on many of his present tasks. In an affluent area like rural Suffolk they might prefer to pay a larger sum to the central funds than work harder for the church.

His wife then appeared with tea and large slabs of fruit cake. As he munched the cake his red cheeks seemed to sag with sadness. I apologized for pointing out all the problems, and said that I was sure a solution could be found. 'Yes,' he replied, and took another bite. I left soon afterwards, promising to keep in touch.

As I drove home I felt very disturbed by my meeting. Here is a man who has a real grasp of what Christian ministry is all about, and who has no ambition other than to serve his people. Yet he feels crushed by the system in which he is forced to operate. And, despite admiring him and being completely in tune with all he said, I actually left him feeling discouraged. There's clearly something wrong with my way of thinking.

29 April 1994

The Bishop of Ely has stayed strangely quiet throughout the Upton saga. During the media blitz he refused all interviews, leaving his PR officer to speak to the cameras. And he has not been in touch with me.

But he's a shrewd man, and I suspect he anticipated something like this. Last summer, before my resignation as vicar took effect, he wrote to me forbidding me to conduct services in Upton and Hamerton after my resignation. I replied – quite honestly – that I always accept invitations to preach from wherever they come, so long as I am available; so he would have to persuade the church-wardens not to invite me. He sent his suffragan bishop to speak to the churchwardens, who listened politely and said that they would invite anyone they chose – myself included.

Upton and Hamerton, without realizing it, are groping their way back to a Saxon, or even Celtic, pattern of church life. The earliest congregations in Britain ran their own affairs, and the members ministered to each other according to their different abilities. Those who were good organizers – like Mike Newton and David Way – managed the material aspects of the church; they leant on the rich to give money to build a new aisle or chancel, and on the poor to dig foundations and mix mortar. Those who were good pastors – like Linda Quinn in Upton or Jessie Swales in Hamerton – ran the spiritual side of church life, drawing out the spiritual gifts of the whole congregation. Those with gifts of healing and encouragement visited the sick and the elderly in the parish. Those with gifts of discernment offered spiritual counsel. Those with gifts of teaching instructed the children. And so on.

Preachers in those days were usually itinerant, travelling from one church to another. They probably realized that listening to the same chap every week, however good he is, eventually becomes boring. Besides, the itinerant preachers could pick up ideas from one church and take them to others; this was the main means by which ideas spread. This is really my vocation; and now that I am free of any management or pastoral role, I can practise it. I can think of a number of other clergy who would be far happier as itinerant preachers than as vicars of a single parish.

Bishops in those days, like Aidan, Cuthbert and Chad, were quite different in style and authority from modern bishops. Stephen Sykes in Ely is in effect chief executive of Ely Diocese PLC: he sits on umpteen committees and allocates jobs to clergy so he has little time, and even less mental and spiritual space, for preaching and teaching – and for the listening to people that the exercise of these gifts requires. Aidan and Cuthbert, by contrast, had no executive power at all. They were apostles who travelled from place to place, talking to people about the gospel and inspiring them to change their lives in accordance with Christ's teaching. They had ample opportunity to listen to the people as well. In addition, they created communities such as Lindisfarne, where people could come and learn more about the gospel and develop their spiritual gifts.

Upton and Hamerton are saying that they don't want a chief executive in Ely running their affairs, but would love an apostle to come from Ely from time to time to inspire them.

4 May 1994

My long love affair with Jesus Christ is only slightly eclipsed by my even longer love affair with the buildings erected in his honour. As an atheist teenager caught up in the hippy scene, I would take every opportunity to slip off alone and wander round medieval churches. My preference was always for remote country churches. I loved – and still love – to work out the story of a church from its stones. Sometimes one can find the ghost of a Saxon window arch in the external wall, or in rare cases an entire Saxon window, the surviving evidence of the earliest stone church which itself replaced an earlier wooden on. Then one can pick out how people in each generation added their own piece to the church or made their own mark: a new aisle; a longer chancel; a set of windows; a high flat root to allow clerestory windows; a tower for bells; a finely carved communion table; a sundial on the south wall; stained glass commemorating local heroes and aristocrats. Although lords of the manor provided much of the money for the work, the ordinary peasants contributed their share through tithes and gifts; and although expert masons and joiners were imported from outside, the local people gave their labour to heave stones and mix mortar. Every church is the embodiment of the community in which it stands – and an expression of its faith.

So just over 10 years ago a group of us started the Cambridgeshire Historic Churches Trust to raise money for churches in dire need, and I have been chairman ever since. During this last decade I have visited innumerable crumbling churches, talked to their clergy and wardens, and tried to guide them in forming a plan for repair. So I have seen the entire business of church conservation from the inside – and I have been appalled. It is controlled by a small group of architects approved by the diocese; and since their fees are proportionate to the cost of repairs, they have an interest in keeping costs high. They in turn seek protection from a small group of specialist builders who, to my certain knowledge, frequently fix the price between themselves. By my reckoning local congregations frequently pay double, or even triple, the amount the repairs really cost.

Two years ago a friend and I started a small firm to do church repairs at cost price. Architects have been very hostile, warning churches against using us; but a few churchwardens are beginning to stand up for themselves, so our work is gradually expanding. Last week I decided to go public. At the annual conference of our Trust, before an audience of 250 – including architects and builders – I gave a lecture exposing the corruption. I doubt if any conference on church conservation has seen anything like it. The majority of the conference – the ordinary people who run jumble sales and garden fêtes for their church roof – cheered. But the architects and builders actually heckled, and finally walked out. I was clearly touching some very raw nerves. Since then the poor postman has again had to bring shoals of letters to our door – mostly very friendly, but a few filled with hate. I have also been told that the Bishop of Ely is very angry.

My own emotions are just as they were two months ago after Upton's decision: both excited and frightened. The institutional church is like a great thick cloth laid over ordinary Christians, which suffocates their faith. So when they see an individual or group tugging at the threads, they feel a surge of hope. That sense of hope for the future excites me. Yet even as we pull at two or three threads, we can see the whole cloth begin to unravel. If Upton became an example which others followed, and if our little building firm set a trend which undermined the central control of church repairs, the potential consequences are huge – and impossible to predict. Those in authority know this, and are fearful, so they react with such fierce hostility. This hostility itself frightens me. And paradoxically I also share their fear: without that cloth we would be free, but we might also feel very chilly.

12 May 1994

I first became involved in Orton Malborne last autumn for my own sake. Having resigned from being a rural vicar I wanted to spend some of my time in a poor urban area. So I telephoned the chairman of a tiny ecumenical congregation on one of the large Peterborough estates, and offered to join their rota of preachers. They have now taken me to their bosom, and, in utterly different circumstances, they are groping towards the same vision of church life as Upton and Hamerton.

Peterborough is an old cathedral city 80 miles north of London which, to its misfortune, was designated 25 years ago as a 'new town' to take excess people from London. Orton Malborne is one of a series of huge 'townships' tacked on to the western side of Peterborough to house this cockney overspill. The architects and planners had a grand scheme of strangely shaped blocks of flats, courtyards and family homes, and large open spaces. But now the communal staircases in the flats are covered with graffiti and smell of urine, and the courtyards and open spaces have become desolate dogs' lavatories. Originally, the Church of England installed a priest, but did not build a church. The priest left four years ago and has not been replaced. And a dwindling congregation of about a dozen people gather each Sunday morning in a tatty community centre. They represent the only Christian presence in the entire estate – so they call themselves the 'Christian Presence'.

When I first got to know them they were still looking to the Church of England – or perhaps the Methodist Church – to provide them with a minister, who – by spiritual magic – would transform them into a thriving, energetic congregation. The Church of England to its shame has been promising that 'one day' it would send a priest. But a few weeks ago I persuaded the archdeacon to admit that this was 'unlikely to happen in the foreseeable future'. I had expected that, when I relayed the news to the congregation, they would be angry or frightened. In fact, there was a communal sigh of relief: now they could get on with working out their own salvation.

Last Sunday after the service I asked the congregation to wait for a moment before getting coffee. And I said that in my view they needed to look from amongst their own number for a leader – a pastor – who would draw out and coordinate their various gifts. I added that, once their own gifts began to be used properly, other people would want to join, and their congregation would begin to grow. One middle-aged man wondered if a pastor was needed: 'Can't we just be a democracy?' To which I answered: 'Yes – your pastor must be democratically elected.' As coffee was being drunk, I heard one or two speculating about who will be chosen as pastor.

There is one obvious candidate, and one dark horse; my money is on the dark horse. The obvious candidate is a Methodist local preacher who has belonged to the congregation since it started. With white hair and beard, speckled with ginger, coming out in thick curls around his face, he looks like an Old Testament prophet. He has managed the church since the priest left, producing a newsletter, arranging people to conduct services and organizing Bible studies. But he is excessively cautious and lacks vision, so he can never take the initiative. The dark horse, Edie, is a Scotswoman who worked as a schools inspector in Peterborough and recently retired. She lives in a private house on a small estate about a mile away, but comes to the Christian Presence because she dislikes large institutional churches. People seem to be a little wary of her, probably because they sense – as I do – that she's someone who enjoys taking risks and trying out new ideas. If so, she is just the kind of pastor we need.

30 July 1994

The Christian Presence in Orton Malborne has no festivals, no seasons. Every Sunday, and even on Christmas Day, the same people turn up, and the service takes the same form. I think this is quite typical of urban churches, large and small. But in Upton the year is punctuated by festivals when the church is full, while on a normal Sunday only a handful come. And undoubtedly the high point of the year is the flower festival on the second weekend of July. Extraordinary artistic talent emerges from the most unexpected people, who devote days of painstaking care to their displays. And on Saturday evening every pew is filled for a Songs of Praise organized by a young woman who hardly appears during the rest of the year.

This year I made a list of all the people who attended, and during the past fortnight I have set aside every afternoon to visit them. My purpose was to listen in depth to their feelings about the step which Upton church made last February and how this step relates to their personal values and beliefs. If Upton's step is simply an internal dispute within the institutional church – about money and power – then it's ultimately pointless. But if in some way it re-connects Christianity with the wider population, it is of profound importance. A large proportion of the village participated in the decision in February – were their hearts really in it?

I've managed to visit about 30 households – and my eyes have been opened. In almost every case we talked quite deeply about matters of faith; far from having to prompt and steer these discussions, people positively wanted to talk about religion. And there was virtual unanimity of view. Yes, all but three people believe in God, and look to Jesus as the perfect example of how people should live. But none of them – not a single one – can make sense of orthodox Christian doctrine. The idea of Jesus as the 'redeemer of mankind' or even the 'Son of God' is completely alien, as is the notion of 'salvation from sin'. I did my best to explain these concepts simply, but only caused people to feel embarrassed, because they felt I was offended by their lack of belief.

If they hadn't already done so, I then took the discussion on to prayer and spiritual experience. Again there was virtual unanimity – in this instance positive. Apart from the three agnostics, they all claim to perceive God's presence in the beauty of nature – so they are happy to speak of God as Creator. They can also sometimes feel God within their own hearts and minds – so God as Spirit is an idea that accords with their experience. A few feel inhibited about talking to God, but most regard this as quite natural, especially in moments of difficulty or crisis.

But in one crucial respect views differ. Those who attend regular services are quite happy to say prayers in which orthodox doctrines are expressed; they regard these doctrines as poetry. This is made easier if the 'old language' of Cranmer's *Book of Common Prayer* is used, since it is so obviously poetic; nonetheless, they do not regard the doctrines as stumbling blocks, even though they do not believe them. The rest – the majority – say that to recite creeds and prayers which you do not accept is hypocritical, and claim that this puts them off regular worship. They are happy to come to the flower festival and to harvest thanksgiving and the carol service at Christmas because these feel like real celebrations of their faith in God and his creation, and in Jesus as the perfect person. But the normal Sunday service feels too solemn.

So how does Upton's step last February fit in with all this? 'It means it's our church again,' they say; 'we can do what we like in it.' That doesn't mean they want bingo nights or riotous parties in church; it is a sacred place in which only sacred things should happen. I think they are expressing something more profound: that church equals God, and if the church belongs to them, they belong to God.

28 August 1994

Richard Titford has come back from holiday and decided to resign from being vicar of his three parishes in Suffolk and apply to be half-time priest, receiving half the stipend.

He now has some delicate negotiating to do. First of all, he must persuade his bishop to support his idea. I expect the bishop will be delighted at the prospect of reducing the salary bill; but the question is whether those parishes will be allowed to pay proportionally less into the central funds. A few years or even months ago such a change would be unthinkable: it was a matter of principle that every parish in the land should be covered by a full-time priest receiving a full salary. But in the present financial crisis bishops will consider anything to make the books balance. So I think Richard will succeed in these negotiations.

Much more difficult will be winning over the parishioners. The English have a strange ambivalence towards the clergy. As George Herbert observed three and a half centuries ago, the clergy are held in fairly low esteem. Most people regard the typical vicar as pleasant and honest, but rather naïve and wimpish. So the clergy project a fairly uninspiring and insipid image of the Christian gospel. Yet equally people find it reassuring to have a vicar in their neighbourhood, and to see him wandering around from time to time. Even if they can't swallow all the doctrines which he apparently believes, and even if they can't emulate his innocent benevolence, they are comforted that such a person exists.

So in Edwardstone, Groton and Little Waldingfield, Richard will have to overcome some deep anxieties, and at the same time foster some quite radical changes of attitude. In particular, he will have to persuade his parishioners that they don't actually need a parson to go from door to door, being faithful and loving on their behalf. On the contrary, they must learn to be more faithful and loving themselves. In fact, he will have to encourage them to take the gospel seriously, as applying directly to them and their behaviour. Richard as a half-time vicar will still be able to conduct services and visit the sick; but he will be much less visible in his parishes, as he will need to be earning half his living elsewhere. In a more gentle and gradual fashion, his parishes will have to follow Upton's example.

The word 'vicar' is actually rather appropriate for what most priests are, but should cease to be. Historically, 'vicar' meant someone who was acting on behalf of a rector. The rector received the income from the parish tithes and glebe, but employed a vicar to do the pastoral work on his behalf. Today it means someone who believes the Christian creed on the people's behalf. Inevitably a vicarious Christian becomes a caricature of the gospel, offering a bland and unchallenging version of the teachings of Jesus. And, whatever their original intentions, most clergy find themselves fitting into this caricature – Richard himself is a good example. If Richard can put his plan into practice, both he and his parishioners will hear and receive the gospel with fresh ears.

18 September 1994

Today, after conducting a service at Hamerton, I was walking up the village street, and met a middle-aged woman who never comes to church. Feeling the need to justify herself, she used the familiar phrase, 'Of course, one can be a good Christian without going to church.' In the past I have always let the phrase pass without comment. But on this occasion I said, 'Yes, of course'. She was utterly nonplussed, and changed the subject.

The reason for my boldness is that I have just been reading the first-ever translation of the letters of Pelagius. He is our one authentic British heretic, whose teaching every theological student is taught to despise. Yet that woman is a true Pelagian, as are many people, including churchgoers – and I am one myself. Pelagius travelled from Britain to Rome in the late fourth century, and acquired a large following; even his opponents admired his personal holiness.

His ideas were really very simple. He believed that human nature is morally neutral, neither good nor evil, but can be directed in good or evil ways; and that Jesus shows us the good way. Individuals are thus free to choose the way of goodness or the way of evil. He regarded prayer not as a means of changing God's mind, causing Him to suspend the laws of nature, but as a source of inward strength: each person has a divine spark, called conscience, which illuminates the way of goodness; and prayer fans this spark into a burning flame. The example he frequently used to illustrate his ideas was ambition. In itself ambition is neither good nor evil; but it can be directed either towards the accumulation of power and wealth, or towards the service of others.

To most people the teaching of Pelagius is common sense. But to the churchmen of his time, especially Augustine of Hippo, it was profoundly dangerous. At heart the reason for their opposition was that Pelagius implicitly challenged the authority of the church. If moral goodness is the route to salvation, and this is a matter of personal choice, then anyone can be saved, regardless of their religion; Jesus is one among many moral teachers who can guide people in the way of goodness. Equally if each person possesses a divine spark, then anyone can learn to pray, regardless of their doctrinal beliefs. In short, it is possible to be a good Christian without going to church, or even believing in Christianity.

Augustine invented a quite different theology which put the institutional church firmly at the centre of things. His key idea was original sin: that the sin of Adam and Eve in eating the apple is passed from one generation to the next, through the sinful act of sex. This means that everyone is condemned to eternal hell. However, God in his mercy sent his Son Jesus Christ to take the punishment on to himself through his death on the cross; and by this means God picks out quite a small number of people for salvation. The institutional church is the means whereby this theology is promulgated, and also the vessel in which the company of the saved is carried to heaven.

Small wonder that many people can't swallow Christian orthodoxy. Augustine won the battle against Pelagius, and his peculiar ideas became official doctrines of the church – and remain so to this day. While, I suspect, few people really believe them, their legacy remains. Christianity is still regarded by many as hostile to sex; and sin is still widely equated with sexual misdemeanour.

The British have never been eager churchgoers: even when it was built in the 14th century, Hamerton church had large empty spaces on Sunday mornings. And the reason is that the British have always been Pelagians at heart. So why bother to keep Hamerton church open now, and put on a service once a fortnight? If we actually tried to close Hamerton church, and sell it off for development as a private house, the lady who never comes to church would bitterly object – as would almost the entire village.

From the start, when the gospel was first preached on these islands, we have been eager to build churches, and to extend and beautify them. Today people are as generous as ever in contributing to church repairs: when I was vicar of Hamerton, the population of 80 people raised £10,000 in less than a year to repair the chancel arch. The building symbolizes in stone the divine spark in the human soul. But as for the services, I'm not so sure. People like to know the services are happening, and even to hear the church bells announcing them, because it reminds them that God is active. But it is vicarious worship – just as vicars provide a kind of vicarious faith. Pelagius wouldn't approve. He would say that if people do not want the services, there is no point in holding them – worship should be judged solely by the degree to which it helps people to choose goodness and to reject evil.

31 October 1994

Anglia Polytechnic University exists in buildings of almost brutal drabness in the midst of one of the finest cities in the world, Cambridge. I lectured there for 13 years until 1990, resigned because I was exhausted, and have now resumed part-time because I need the money. To my surprise I am enjoying it, and feel stimulated and refreshed by being amongst people who – for the most part – know virtually nothing about Christianity.

Economists like me are supposed to be totally indifferent to religion; indeed, in most people's eyes, religion and economics are at opposite ends of the spectrum of human experience. So my students are a little surprised when I introduce myself, at the start of the first lecture, as a disciple of Jesus Christ. When I began lecturing in 1977 most youngsters still had a working knowledge of Christianity: they had sung hymns and learnt Bible stories at school. That was even true in the late 1980s. But those now emerging into adulthood comprise the first generation for 15 centuries to whom the Christian faith is utterly alien. The other day in a tutorial I referred to a person as 'a good Samaritan', and the students asked me what I meant.

I don't feel sad or angry about this; I don't want to rail at trendy teachers for failing to drum spiritual values into their pupils. As the child of atheist parents who warned me against taking divinity classes too seriously, I feel that the irreligious – or non-religious – mind is far more receptive to the gospel than the mind which has been fed since childhood with religious maxims and images. Jesus himself tried to redeem people from the stultifying religion of his time, so that they could encounter the truth for themselves. People flocked to Jesus because they were hungry for the spiritual bread he gave; and I sense in many of my students the same spiritual hunger.

What grieves me is that the churches are quite unable to reach the great majority of these young people; on the contrary, in so far as the young are aware that Christianity exists, the churches contrive to give the impression that Jesus Christ is utterly irrelevant to their lives. It's not the buildings that put them off. In fact, by sleight of hand I managed last week to steer a tutorial discussion on to the subject of church architecture, and I was amazed at the enthusiasm expressed for our great cathedrals and parish churches. My students' attitude is similar, though not as strong, as my own at their age: despite my atheism I loved wandering round medieval churches, sensing that their sublime beauty expressed profound truth about the human condition.

The real problem with the churches is, as one might expect, the religion they peddle. Young people see the churches as finger-wagging organizations, stipulating a particular creed and set of moral values, and castigating those who do not comply. A minority, who find security in conforming to beliefs and morals handed down from on high, are attracted; and even Anglia Polytechnic University has a small Christian Union, representing a third of one per cent of the student body. But most regard this kind of religion with contempt, and look elsewhere for spiritual nourishment. At the student fair a fortnight ago, when the various societies try to lure new members, Buddhism, two varieties of Hinduism, and an alternative healing group were all doing brisk business. And the Friends of the Earth, whose stall was besieged by enquiries, has in my view a strong spiritual dimension: people want to conserve the environment not just for human benefit, but because they recognize the spiritual unity of all creation.

If we brought economics and religion together, and treated the different religions like supermarket chains, the answer would be simple. A few years ago Tesco seemed dowdy and dull, with its sales gradually declining; then it changed its image and its products completely, and now it's about to overtake Sainsbury's. If Tesco can do it, so can Christianity. In fact, it should be easier for Christianity. We don't need to invent a new image; we only need to present Jesus Christ and his gospel as they really are, and my young students would soon start taking notice.

18 November 1994

This afternoon I was entertained to cappuccino and chocolate cake at Tatties by four students who wanted to talk about Christianity. They invited me at the end of last week's lecture on European monetary integration.

'What do you really believe?' they asked. They had been intrigued by a throwaway remark I had made in a lecture about Christianity being an excellent faith for agnostics.

'I believe nothing,' I replied.

'So how can you be a Christian?'

'Because Jesus Christ doesn't require me to believe anything; he invites me to discover things.'

This led to a long discussion about the nature of faith. I explained that I had become a disciple of Jesus Christ in 1970, while I was still an agnostic. I had read the gospels, interpreting the word 'God' as meaning human perfection, and 'heaven' as the joy of being perfect. And having surmounted this theological stumbling block, I was able to encounter Jesus for the first time as he really was. I described to the four students my response: I was captivated by this enigmatic, rebellious, witty, passionate, poetic man who wandered through the dusty lanes of Palestine. I fell in love with him, and I decided to make him my spiritual teacher for an experimental period of six months.

'So do you believe in God now?'

'No, I don't believe in God as a kind of intellectual proposition. But I have come to sense an objective being, a spirit, present in all creation and within my heart, who radiates love.'

'And where does this sense come from?'

'From following the instructions of Jesus.'

I described how I had begun to pray and meditate, simply because Jesus taught this. At first I had imagined that prayer was a kind of psychological technique, but increasingly I came to 'know

God' as a reality, both within the psyche and beyond. Three of the four students could understand from their own experience what I was talking about. In a very informal way they had all meditated – usually when listening to music or walking in the country – and had sensed the divine reality unifying all creation. The fourth student was still kicking his feet against the theological stumbling block. He alone had been taken to church as a boy, and couldn't understand how it was possible to know God without believing in Him – it didn't fit the intellectual framework he had acquired at Sunday School. So although he had rejected that framework, he was stuck on the idea that to be religious he needed to accept it again.

Then we got on to morals – or, rather, sex. 'Can a Christian have sex before marriage?' 'Can Christians be gay?' 'Is AIDS God's judgment on immorality?' When students of my generation asked these questions they were deadly serious, and their behaviour was influenced by the answers they reached. These students – two boys and two girls – were testing me to see whether Christianity can possibly relate to the modern sexual scene, or whether it is stuck in some cultural and moral ghetto. Instead of answering their questions directly, I asked them about their sexual morals. They believe in sexual fidelity in the sense that a person should have only one sexual partner at a time. They are not disapproving about people changing partners, but they regard a life-long relationship as the ideal. And they think the same morality should apply equally to gays and straights.

Then I asked them about the basis for their moral views. One – the former Sunday School attender – argued that all morality is determined by culture and upbringing, so in an objective sense there is no right or wrong. The other three said that, while culture plays a part, there are some basic moral principles inherent within the human psyche – just as animals and birds seem to behave according to certain principles. And they said that sexual fidelity is one of these principles; human beings naturally want to be faithful. So I replied that they had answered their own questions. The moral teaching of Jesus is not something to be imposed on people; rather, he illuminated, in the most vivid phrases and stories, the basic moral principles which – in Paul's words – are 'written on every human heart'.

By the time we had all finished a second cappuccino, the tables were full, and it was time to leave. I thanked the students for their hospitality, and said that I had no wish to persuade them to become Christians for its own sake. 'I just want you to lead full and good lives,' I concluded, 'and I commend Jesus as an excellent guide.' The ex-Sunday School pupil seemed angry at these words, as if I was letting him down: he had come to hate Christianity, but still wanted it served to him in the orthodox, Sunday School form. The others were palpably relieved, and thanked me profusely for our conversation; I had allowed them to take Jesus Christ seriously.

22 December 1994

'The trouble with Upton is that most of the people involved with the church aren't Anglican.' So said one of the clergy from a nearby parish when I met him at a Christmas party. He is absolutely right. Of the seven members of the church council only two are solid members of the Church of England; four are Catholic or Nonconformist by background; and one is, by his own admission, 'not very religious' but loves the church building and the festivals. A similar lack of Anglicans can be found amongst the people who attend occasionally and supported the decision to rebel.

Undoubtedly this has had an important influence on Upton's stance. A congregation whose members had all been brought up within the C of E, and absorbed its hierarchical ethos since childhood, would have found it impossible to envisage life without a vicar, and would have been far more reluctant to defy the authorities. Yet Upton's mongrel mix is increasingly typical of rural churches. In towns and suburbs people still have a range of different churches and chapels to choose from; so Catholics can worship in the RC church, Anglicans in the C of E church, and Nonconformists can conform to their nonconformity. But in most villages the chapels have closed and only the parish church remains, so people who wish to worship within their community must go to the parish church – which, owing to Henry VIII's marital confusions, belongs now to the C of E. So it's small wonder that rebellion against the system should come first in the countryside.

Yet there is another sense in which Upton is being more truly ecumenical – and more truly British – than the bishops and archdeacons who react to it so fiercely. In Upton, like Hamerton, they use and love Cranmer's *Prayer Book*. This is not just because they love the exquisite old language, but because they recognize that it recalls a Christian vision to which they aspire. Cranmer took the ancient monastic daily offices, and simplified them into a pattern of daily and weekly worship in which everyone could participate. Thus he democratized worship: it was no longer a matter for specialists – monks, nuns and priests – but for ordinary people. Indeed, he clearly intended that families should gather in their own homes, or in the parish church, to say Matins and Evensong, with one of the menfolk leading the service, and others reading the lessons.

Whether or not he realized it, Cranmer stood firmly in a tradition that goes right back to Saxon and Celtic times. In preparation for a lecture course next term on economic history, I've just re-read Sidney and Beatrice Webb's glorious book on the history of government in Britain – a source of the kind of lateral insight with which I try to pepper my lectures. They describe the parish church in ancient times as 'the cradle of democracy'. Long before the national parliament was elected, local people were voting for their own churchwardens, sextons and beadles. And, in cooperation with the lord of the manor, they chose their own pastors, sending them off as necessary to be trained in the Bible. Thus not only was worship democratic, but so was every other aspect of parish life.

The Nonconformists in Upton church understand the democratic spirit instinctively. After all, the various Nonconformist churches – Baptist, Congregationalists, Methodists and so on – broke away in the 17th and 18th centuries because the bishops and priests were trying to reassert control. And, in a strange way, the Catholics are also more democratic in approach. Over the past two centuries the RC Church in England has rebuilt itself through the commitment and vision of the ordinary members, many of whom had little or no education; and the Second Vatican Council in the 1960s affirmed the clergy and laity together – the 'whole people of God' – as the ultimate source of authority.

And I, too, am an instinctive democrat – though in my case it is not because of my religious background, but my lack of it. Secular, liberal values were taken for granted in my atheist family; and the undemocratic authority of bishops and clergy, insofar as we ever discussed it, was simply mocked as absurd and anachronistic. It was an article of faith for both my mother and my father that you should be 'no respecter of persons': you should treat everyone with equal respect regardless of their status or position. In my various encounters with bishops over the years I have always sensed a clash of values, or at least a degree of tension. They expect to be treated with special respect due to their office, and most clergy and laity become horribly deferential in their presence. But I cannot treat them as anything other than fallible individuals trying to do a particular job. And the trouble is that the job, as currently understood, is both misconceived in principle and impossible in practice – hence Upton's rebellion.

1 January 1995

'Come unto me all ye who are heavy laden . . . my yoke is easy, my burden is light.' I am sitting within the heavy gloom of Sheffield Cathedral. Sarah's and my idea of a post-Christmas holiday is to visit a large city and imbibe its atmosphere. We have just been on the eerily smooth new tram to the vast shopping complex on the edge of the city, which is built in a glorious caricature of a Greek temple, with a dazzling array of Doric, Tuscan and Corinthian columns made from fibre-glass. Now we are waiting for a Communion service in half an hour's time to celebrate the naming of Jesus: we have communed with the god of consumerism, now we will commune with the God of love. The trouble is that the consumerist god has a much jollier and light-hearted place of worship.

The religion which Jesus struggled against – the religion peddled by the scribes, Pharisees and Sadducees – was horribly solemn, putting huge spiritual, moral and material burdens on people's shoulders. The most obvious burdens were moral. In primitive tribal society the old Hebrew laws made sense, but in the more sophisticated, and to some degree urban, civilization of first-century Palestine most of the laws were anachronistic. Instead of discarding them, the scribes and Pharisees turned the laws into tests of religious devotion. They prided themselves on their minute knowledge and observance of every law, and insisted that others followed their example, reprimanding those who failed. So most ordinary people passed through life with a burden of guilt on their backs. And, in many people's eyes, Christianity is no better. Christian leaders seem smug and self-satisfied because they manage to keep the moral rules, and they try and make others feel guilty for failing. Small wonder that people cheer when a bishop or vicar slips up.

The scribes and Pharisees also placed doctrinal burdens on

people. The religion of the Old Testament is remarkably free of doctrines. Apart from belief in God, there is virtually no theology from one end to the other – not even much speculation about life after death. But by the time of Jesus, largely under Greek influence, Judaism was crawling with theology. And, as always happens when theology gets going, they had divided into different sects according to their different theological systems, the Pharisees and Sadducees being the leading groups. Again Christianity has inherited this obsession with doctrine, developing an elaborate system of theology which is deemed 'orthodox', and condemning those who do not subscribe to it as 'heretical'. And predictably it has had a long succession of quarrels and divisions over obscure doctrinal formulae. So in most people's eyes to be a Christian is a matter of believing a whole set of propositions that can never be proved.

There were worship burdens too which led, in turn, to financial burdens. The Judaism in which Jesus grew up had become a maze of complex rituals, which required an army of priests to conduct. The ordinary Jew not only had to attend these rituals, but also contribute large sums to pay the priests and maintain the synagogues and temples in which the rituals took place. In its medieval heyday Christian ritual had become even more complex, and its clerical army even more numerous and costly. Today, happily, the rituals are much simpler. Yet the 'practising' Christian can still spend many hours each week at services, at fund-raising activities and, most of all, at meetings to arrange these activities. The church remains a very time-consuming and expensive organization.

Any religion which develops to become a large institution is bound to create these burdens for its members. It must prescribe rules for its members to follow, and creeds for its members to believe, because only in this way can it maintain its integrity and coherence. And it must employ large numbers of staff to manage itself. So, while Christians insist on belonging to these institutions, they must carry these burdens.

By the time Jesus appeared, the Jewish religion and its various sects had become distinctly unpopular. The leaders were despised, and the doctrines and morals they peddled were resented.

So when Jesus declared 'my yoke is easy and my burden is light', people flocked to hear him. And as they listened to his words they could feel the burdens falling from their shoulders. He replaced moral rules with the spirit of love, doctrinal formulae with the direct experience of truth; and, in doing so, he abolished the need for large religious institutions.

Why do we so persistently betray this wonderful vision of lightness, and place burdens on each other's shoulders?

10 January 1995

In Upton and Hamerton the people have to assert their autonomy from diocesan control, in the teeth of bitter opposition. In Africa each local church has no choice but to be autonomous, because communications are so poor that central control is impossible.

Yesterday we received a delightful letter from Sam Kokini, one of the Sudanese pastors my wife and I are supporting. We have made a link with a tribal group on the border of Sudan and Uganda, visiting them on two occasions. We raise money to support pastors there, and also to train young men in building skills so they can reconstruct the schools and hospitals that have been destroyed in the civil war. The people of Upton and Hamerton are wonderfully generous – and have become more so since they stopped paying their diocesan quota to Ely.

Sam's story could have been that of a Celtic pastor 13 hundred years ago. He grew up in a remote village about 50 miles north of the border, where Christianity was virtually unknown. One day a group of evangelists from the town of Yei arrived in the village, and a number of people, including Sam, embraced the gospel. They began to meet each Sunday for worship, and eventually built a small church out of bamboos and banana leaves. Then Sam – that was the name he adopted at baptism – and another man were chosen to be pastors. The people raised funds to send them to Yei for training, and two years later Sam and his friend returned. Through their efforts, the Christian community grew rapidly, and almost every year they had to pull down the existing church and build a bigger one. Sadly in 1990 this village was raided by government forces and the whole village fled southwards. But they have now built a new village, including a church, nearer the border.

Sam's letter describes a visit from their bishop, Seme Solomone. We have met Seme on both our visits to the area. He is a cross between a tribal chief and a saint. He is tall and broad, and by Sudanese standards hugely fat. Despite the chronic famine there, the local people organize feasts wherever he goes, so he eats very well. When he arrives in a village the people fall at his feet, and he blesses them. Yet despite his full stomach he is willing to endure any discomfort or danger in order to visit the churches in his diocese. Indeed, he specifically tries to visit places where the civil war is at its fiercest, so he can offer comfort and encouragement. And this is why he came to Sam's village: government planes have been dropping bombs in the locality, and their ground forces are gradually approaching.

Sam and his people had no warning of the bishop's visit, because there is no post or telephone. But as soon as Seme arrived three calves were slaughtered and hundreds of pancakes baked; and overnight a large awning was constructed of banana leaves in the centre of the village. The following day a service lasting three hours was held under the awning, followed by a feast. At both the service and the feast the bishop spoke, comparing the suffering of the people now with that of Christ on the cross, and urging them to retain faith and courage until peace and harmony would rise again in their land. As Sam recognizes, there was nothing new or original in what the bishop said: 'He was simply preaching the gospel which we have heard many times before. But he spoke with great warmth and conviction. And we were so pleased that he had taken such trouble to come and see us.' Sam concludes: 'We had great joy in the name of the Lord Jesus. Everyone in the village came, and during the service fifteen people became Christians, stepping forward to declare their faith in Christ. Even the aeroplanes above our heads could not spoil our happiness.' That evening he wrote this letter to us, and asked Bishop Seme to post it.

Apart from the aeroplanes it could have been a scene in Northumbria when Cuthbert visited one of his new churches, or Essex when Cedd arrived from his monastery in Bradwell. Could it be repeated in Britain today? Seme and Sam look to the Church of England as their mother church, because English missionaries brought the gospel to Sudan early this century. Now the mother must learn the faith afresh from the daughter. It is tempting to say that modern British people are too sophisticated and well-educated to emulate the simple faith of the African tribespeople. Yet while our material lives may be horribly complex, in spiritual matters we are as naïve as illiterate peasants. The problem is that Christianity, as presented in Britain today, is not simple enough: it has too much theology and morality, and too many layers of government. Sam's church is successful because it is a simple organization with a simple message about love, forgiveness and joy. Our churches are failing because they belong to a complicated organization with a message few can understand, and even fewer can accept.

19 January 1995

'He's a splendid fellow,' my aristocratic Norfolk friend pronounced. 'He has ten churches which are all in good nick; and he even finds time to visit the sick.' It was an unintended rhyming couplet which stuck in my mind. Then she added: 'But now the silly idiot wants to get married for a third time, so the bishop's sacked him. Can't he just have a discreet affair?'

The 'silly idiot' is Kit Chalcraft, and his 10 parishes are in the southwest corner of Norfolk, near Swaffham, an area I've never visited. At first, I thought little of that brief conversation just before Christmas. Despite prating on about 'the sanctity of Christian marriage' – as if a Christian marriage was different from any other kind – the clergy are as prone to marital discord as any other group. My main interest was to hear that in Norfolk they now have 10 churches per vicar, while in Cambridgeshire four or five is still the norm. So I began to speculate idly about Kit Chalcraft's typical Sunday. After a blazing row with his wife, he sets off in a red sports car to dash from church to church, managing to get through Holy Communion in an average of 22 minutes and 34 seconds. Or perhaps he has installed a video machine on each altar, showing him celebrating Communion; the churchwardens place bread and wine in front of the screen, and at the appropriate moment come up and help themselves.

But now the churchwardens from southwest Norfolk have contacted me for advice. They have heard about events in Upton and Hamerton, and wonder if our experience may be relevant to them; so they have asked me to come and meet them in 10 days' time. And this afternoon a journalist from BBC Television came to see me, asking if I would participate in a half-hour documentary about the 'Kit Chalcraft affair'. From the journalist I have gleaned the story so far.

Kit Chalcraft was a vicar in a group of parishes near Norwich.

Then his wife went on an Open University summer school, I found out later, and – following a well-trodden path that should be described in the OU prospectus – fell in love with a fellow student. After six years of divided loyalty, she left the vicarage to move in with her new man, divorcing her husband. Following this trauma, he made a disastrous remarriage, which was doomed within months, I subsequently discovered. According to the twisted logic which the C of E applies in such cases, the bishop required Kit Chalcraft and his new wife to move to another set of parishes. So in 1989 he arrived in the Breckland area of southwest Norfolk. The churchwardens generously supported him when his second wife left him.

But he was now utterly devastated, and became deeply depressed. Yet in the meantime he proved himself to be a superb pastor. He was tireless in visiting people in the parish, and almost everyone liked him. When anyone was in distress, he seemed always to have the right words to comfort and uplift them. If a sick or elderly person needed a lift to hospital, either he would take them himself, or arrange for someone else to do so. And he had a gift for discerning the spiritual gifts in his congregations, and encouraged people to develop and use their gifts. Indeed, many people were struck by his natural humility, so that, unlike many clergy, he could enable others to take roles traditionally filled by priests – such as preaching and visiting the sick – without feeling threatened.

At this point the BBC Television producer became a little sheepish: 'I have to say that I have been amazed at how highly people speak of him. I've never known a vicar to be so popular.' He then continued the story. About three years ago Kit ran into an old friend, Susie Hall, in a supermarket in Swaffham. They had known each other for 20 years – their families were from the same parish. Susie had been a television presenter, but after her husband's premature death had given up her career, and had retired to a lovely Georgian house in the town. The relationship blossomed and they decided to marry, to the delight of family and friends.

The producer was now rather vague about the precise sequence of events. For reasons he could not fathom, the Bishop of Norwich, who had allowed the second marriage, refused to allow the third. But it had taken him at least a year to reach this decision. And having reached it, he became angrily hostile towards Kit, and tried to sack him. After the intervention of lawyers the dismissal has been delayed until the end of next month. Most of the churchwardens and the local people are apparently furious, and all sorts of dire threats are flying around. Hence a television documentary to get to the bottom of it all.

It's clearly a story that makes Upton seem like the proverbial vicarage tea party: anger and sex rolled into one. I feel cautious. I don't feel it's my business to defend Kit Chalcraft against the bishop, or even to justify the bishop's actions to Kit Chalcraft. Since I believe pastors should primarily be answerable to their congregations, it is for the congregations to make a stand if they feel their pastor is being unjustly treated. Yet I sense that this case is not just about Kit Chalcraft; it is about the much deeper issues of ministry and management which led to Upton's rebellion.

28 January 1995

I felt like the detective in an Agatha Christie story entering the scene of a murder. It was a large, rambling farmhouse, with one room leading to the next. The owner, Cyril Lake, is short, broad and plump, with a mischievous grin and large, rough farmer's hands; his wife Dot is the same shape with a sweet innocent smile. They sat at either end of the large oak dining table. The other characters at the table were a retired Home Service announcer who has the kind of clipped, yet mellifluous baritone voice that once filled the airwaves; a Welsh chartered surveyor with a swift, clever mind that could out-manoeuvre any bishop; an army major's widow, who regards the entire ecclesiastical hierarchy as 'an absolute shambles'; a flamboyant artist and antiques dealer, who, many years ago had been a male model appearing in illustrations for knitting patterns; and a delightful elderly farmer with a wicked twinkle and a thick Norfolk accent who demanded from time to time a 'strong dose of common sense'.

At the start each of these characters told me their account of recent events. From what I could gather Kit had tried and failed to get an interview with his diocesan bishop, Peter Nott, in order to tell him of his liaison with Susie Hall, and she had similarly been refused a meeting. Both were fobbed off with the assistant bishop who told them that marriage would be difficult, but if they continued their relationship with discretion, there was no reason for Kit to have to give up his ministry – particularly as the church-wardens and parishioners were clearly anxious for him to remain with them, and only too pleased to see their vicar so happy.

Then, for reasons no one can understand, the bishop summoned Kit Chalcraft about a year ago. The diocesan lawyer was present, and the bishop demanded that Kit should sign a legal document which in effect was a promise to break his relationship with Susie Hall. Kit Chalcraft refused, asking that his own lawyer become involved. A form of words was eventually hammered out that was manifestly ambiguous: Kit undertook to live alone at the rectory, but no mention was made of his paying visits to Susie Hall's home in Swaffham; it was also agreed that in the event of their marrying, he would have to resign his job.

'Kit's been completely honest with us all along,' said Cyril.

'Yes, he told us that he and Susie saw themselves as married in spirit,' added Dot.

'And he said that if we didn't like them going on like this, we only needed to tell him, and he would resign,' continued Cyril.

'But we did,' continued Dot, meaning that they did like him treating Susie as his wife.

'Marriage isn't a bit of paper or even a service in church,' said the major's widow. 'It's about two people loving each other and caring for each other. And Kit and Susie love each other just as much as my husband and I did for fifty years.'

'That's what I call common sense,' pronounced the farmer.

Would they take such an open and generous attitude, I wonder, if they weren't so devoted to Kit?

But then a few months ago it came to the attention of the bishop that Kit had spent nights in Swaffham. The bishop summoned Kit again, and sacked him for failing to keep his promise. Kit protested that he had kept his promise, but to no avail. Kit's dismissal takes effect from the end of next month.

The churchwardens were furious, and demanded to see the bishop, who invited them to his palace. A tense and acrimonious discussion took place, at the end of which the bishop produced a draft press release for them to sign, declaring their support for his actions. This proved fatal. 'What on earth is the point of our coming to see you,' they shouted, 'if you've decided the outcome in advance?' Almost all refused to sign.

Since the story so far had now been fully related, Dot left the room, and shortly afterwards reappeared with a huge pot of tea and five large cakes. As we munched and slurped, I told the story of Upton, and suggested they could take a similar course. Kit could still remain involved, visiting people and even conducting some services. But the churchwardens and church councils would manage their respective churches and organize the various aspects of church life; and if they wished to make some payment to Kit, it would be a private matter between them.

'Would we still have to pay our quota to the diocese?' one of them asked.

'That is up to you,' I replied. 'It is in law a purely voluntary payment.' And I added that Upton no longer paid its quota, but instead set money aside to help poorer churches in the cities. 'That sounds like common sense to me,' said the farmer.

7 February 1995

This afternoon a camera crew is coming to my house to interview me about my reaction to the 'Kit Chalcraft affair', as it has become known. I feel horribly muddled. A number of quite separate threads have got tangled up, and I don't know how to untangle them.

The most conspicuous thread, which has greatest interest for the television cameras, is sex. Should a person who has been married twice and wants to marry a third time be allowed to continue as a vicar? Should a man who admits to having a sexual relationship with a woman before marrying her be stripped of his priesthood? The trouble is that I don't believe in priests, in the sense of people in dog collars who represent God and channel His grace. A central tenet of Christ's teaching is that every person can have a direct, personal relationship with God, so priests are unnecessary. Also, like the major's widow, I don't believe marriage is about legal bits of paper, but is about the quality of love and fidelity between two people. And the fact that someone has failed twice shouldn't prevent a third attempt; repentance and forgiveness are also central tenets. I have not yet met either Kit or Susie; but if they have already committed themselves to stay together for better and for worse, then I'm sure God already blesses their union.

Another thread is about ministry. I think most people share my scepticism about priesthood, yet equally they like to have a vicar around. To some extent they just want someone to be Christian on their behalf. But that's not how the churchwardens in Norfolk see things. They take their faith far too seriously to need anyone else to be faithful for them. Yet they recognize that pastorship – visiting people, encouraging them, discerning their gifts – is a special ministry on which the other aspects of the church's ministry depends. So they want someone who possesses the gift of pastorship, and has sufficient time to act as pastor to their parishes. They emphatically don't want a full-time manager to 'run the parishes'; they are more than capable of doing this themselves. Kit, by all accounts, is a first-rate pastor and an incompetent manager; that's why they want to keep him.

A third thread is money. Today we enjoy affluence beyond the wildest dreams of our medieval or even Victorian ancestors. They managed to build cathedrals and churches, and then continuously extend and enhance them; to support their pastors; and set aside land and other capital to endow both the buildings and the pastors. So in Upton and Hamerton, in the Breckland area of Norfolk, and in most other parts of Britain, there is ample money to keep those buildings in good repair and to pay salaries to pastors – despite the large losses incurred by the Church Commissioners. The problem centres on control and this is really what the Norfolk rebellion is about. They can happily maintain their buildings because the task is largely in their hands. But people are very reluctant to pay money into a central fund for clergy salaries – especially if they have virtually no influence on who is appointed, how many parishes he is supposed to cover, and what work he is to do. That is why the people in Norfolk, like those in Upton, are objecting to the quota.

These may be the first uncertain stirrings of an anti-colonial revolt. In America the issue which triggered the revolution was a tax on tea; here it is the sacking of a much-loved pastor. But in both cases the issue is the same: people want to control their own destiny. Today we take freedom for granted as a basic political value. These people in Norfolk are struggling to discover what freedom means within the church. This perhaps is what I must talk about on television.

22 February 1995

I arrived home at 5 o'clock to find seven messages on my answering machine, of which six were from Breckland church-wardens. The Bishop of Norwich has announced that on the evening of 1 March, the day after Kit Chalcraft's dismissal takes effect, he is to appoint the local archdeacon, Tony Foottit, as priest of the 10 parishes. What should they do?

This is the moment of decision for us all. The bishop has clearly decided to call their bluff. Normally in Norfolk, when a vicar leaves, there is a two- or three-year gap before a new one is appointed; indeed lots of dioceses now use this ploy to save money. So by appointing someone immediately the bishop is trying to stamp out the incipient rebellion. Tony Foottit will apparently function as part-time vicar for three or six months, while a permanent man is found.

I believe that the bishop's actions within canon law would be open to question. Even when appointing a temporary priest the bishop has an obligation to consult the churchwardens; and when making a permanent appointment the churchwardens can even veto the bishop's choice. I will check this with David Way later tonight when he returns home from London. As churchwarden of Hamerton, David is a staunch defender of tradition; indeed, like me, he would like to return to Cranmer's original prayer book, abandoning the rather poor revision of 1662. And he is delighted to use his immense legal skills to defend the historic rights of churchwardens and local people to uphold the old custom. It takes his kind of mind to interpret modern canon laws, designed to increase the powers of bishops to have the opposite effect.

If David confirms my hunch about canon law, the church-wardens have the right simply to refuse to accept Tony Foottit as their priest. My impression at the meeting last month is that the churchwardens of the various churches may divide at this point.

Almost everyone would like to keep Kit Chalcraft as vicar, but only about half the parishes are willing to defy the bishop. The question now is whether they will take their defiance to its logical conclusion. The conflict is reaching a climax far sooner than any of us anticipated.

If the churchwardens stand firm, I will be faced with an even harder decision. They have told me that, whatever happens, Kit is so bruised by recent events that he will lie low for some months after his dismissal. Thus they will need someone immediately to conduct services. In his telephone message the Welsh land agent, John Davies, suggests that I might fit the bill. If I accept this suggestion I will be openly defying the Bishop of Norwich. I wrote out of courtesy to Peter Nott in January to tell him of my contacts with the churchwardens in Breckland, and received an extremely abrupt letter in reply. So the chances of his gracefully allowing me to support a rebellion against him are less than zero. In principle my own bishop could react by 'defrocking' me.

Of course, I must pray about all this. And I daresay Peter Nott is praying also. Unfortunately this doesn't mean that we'll reach the same conclusion. My spiritual ears are too deaf ever to hear clear guidance from God; and I doubt if Bishop Nott is any better attuned to the Almighty. I hope that whatever I decide to do, I will be filled with honest doubt, and so admit the possibility that I might be wrong. If Peter Nott feels the same, reconciliation will eventually occur.

In the meantime I must reply to all the messages on the machine. I will tell them that in my opinion they would be within their legal rights to refuse Tony Foottit as priest; and that I will draft for them a letter to the bishop, outlining their legal position. They will then have to make up their own minds.

26 February 1995

For the past month Kit Chalcraft, and the consequences of his actions, have dominated my life; and seemingly he will continue to affect me profoundly for months and perhaps years to come. Now at last I have met him. He stayed with us last night, and we spent the evening reflecting on the extraordinary situation he has unwittingly created.

I can see why the parishes are so keen on him. The newspapers have dubbed him a 'randy vicar'; in fact, he has a rather innocent, other-worldly air about him. He is tall and gangling, dressed in old crumpled clothes that are either too big or too small for him. He has a mischievous twinkle in his eyes, like that of a schoolboy who constantly plays pranks, and the up-turned snub nose of a child. And he speaks with the slight hesitancy of a shy youngster, in a high-pitched, almost plaintive tone. Every now and again his face creases, and when he laughs he emanates a noise between a whistle and a scream with each intake of breath.

Throughout our conversation he wanted to stress the qualities which he respects and admires in everyone he referred to, and seems genuinely to regard most people as better and more talented than himself. But when the discussion turned to the bishop, his expression darkened, his voice dropped, and his whole body became tense. He doesn't feel bitter or angry towards Peter Nott. His reaction is like that of a child who has been punished unjustly: he is both deeply hurt and utterly bewildered. He related all his various dealings with the bishop and his underlings over the past three years to demonstrate his honesty throughout: 'I have told the bishop more than I've told my own mother about my relationship with Susie.' And he says that if the bishop had simply asked him to resign quietly in order to marry Susie, as he had first planned to do, he would have done so without fuss. But he cannot understand why the bishop felt it necessary to sack him in such a peremptory and cold-hearted fashion. One particular phrase of the bishop's in their final meeting sticks in his throat: 'I know you're popular in those parishes – your whole ministry is about courting popularity.'

I turned the conversation towards Kit's personal faith. He describes himself as 'evangelical'. He readily speaks of Jesus Christ as 'my Master and Saviour', and he has a passionate devotion for Christ. I said that evangelicals tend to have rather strict views about marriage; so how did he square this with his own marital experience? 'Evangelicals have even stricter views about forgiveness,' he replied. He related how his two previous marriages went wrong. He didn't blame his wives, although in both cases they walked out on him. Rather, he blamed himself: 'I gave so much love to my parishioners, and got so bound up emotionally with their problems, that I had too little love left for my family.'

'So perhaps it is just as well that you will no longer be a vicar when you marry Susie,' I ventured.

'But Susie shares my love for the parishioners,' he replied, 'so the parishes would unite us more closely.'

'How do you see your future ministry?' I asked.

'I don't know,' he answered forlornly.

'Will you continue to visit people in the parishes?'

'Oh yes; you see, they are my friends.'

'How about conducting worship?'

'I won't be allowed to; the bishop won't give his permission.'

'Why not ignore the bishop, and do what you think is right?'

'I hadn't thought of that.'

Yes, Kit is a child who desperately wants the approval of his elders and betters. But his elders and betters have decided to throw him out of the house, shouting at him never to return. He must now struggle with himself and his faith. Until now he has too readily equated those in authority within the Church with God; and so he has assumed that if he keeps their rules and performs well in the job they give him, he will have obeyed God's will. In other words, he has been guilty of the kind of idolatry which created the institutional Church in the first place, and continues to hold it together. Now the idols have shown themselves to be flawed.

2 March 1995

While I lay quietly in bed last night my answering machine filled up with descriptions of the evening's events; and having now rung back some of the callers, I have a fairly clear impression of what occurred.

The church porch was surrounded by television cameras and radio microphones, and illuminated by spotlights on metal stakes. The bishop and his chaplain processed in, followed by the archdeacon, Tony Foottit. There were a couple of hymns and some prayers, and then the bishop came forward to the chancel steps facing the congregation. He read the legal form of words announcing his intention to 'license' the archdeacon as temporary priest for the 10 parishes. When he had finished, Cyril Lake rose up, marched to the front, and faced the bishop. With his hands and his voice shaking, he began to read out a statement saying that five of the parishes – Oxborough, Threxton, Didlington, Little Cressingham and Bodney – refused to accept Mr Foottit as priest, and that the licensing was illegal. But before Cyril had finished, the bishop turned his back and walked to the altar. He then nodded to his chaplain to announce the next hymn, and the chaplain prodded the organist – a middle-aged lady called Doreen – to start playing. So Cyril was drowned out. He walked to the door, and was followed by the other members of the five rebel parishes.

The service apparently continued with Holy Communion. But people from the conformist parishes who remained had been so horrified by the bishop's rudeness that only three were willing to receive the bread and wine from his hands. As soon as the service was over, Doreen rushed home to fetch her husband, a big burly man with large white sideburns. Furious at the way his wife had been prodded, and furious too that his wife had been forced to interrupt their old friend Cyril, he sped to the church and demanded that the bishop apologize. The bishop, who is small and

51

slight, stuttered a few graceless words of remorse, and then headed for his car.

Throughout this saga the bishop has underestimated the moral strength and determination of the churchwardens. He is so accustomed to being treated with deference wherever he goes that he cannot believe that mere lay people will stand up against him. Having been a bishop for 17 years – first in Somerset and now in Norfolk – he has come to see his mitre and crozier, and his bright purple shirt, as protection against criticism. Yet an old Norfolk farmer like Cyril will 'bend the knee to no man'; and he will respect only those people who have earned respect by their behaviour, not merely by their office.

Yet I can't help but feel a little sorry for the bishop. Like Kit, he must possess a kind of naïve innocence. Anyone with the slightest understanding of the modern media would have known that his actions last night were a public relations disaster: in the eyes of the world – the television cameras – he made an utter fool of himself. Cyril by contrast is a natural media star: his weather-beaten face and his round Norfolk vowels radiate honesty and sincerity. The bishop only needed to hear Cyril out, then politely ask him to resume his seat, and the whole protest would have been deflated. But perhaps I am wrong to think of the bishop as innocent. He was simply being true to himself – just as Cyril was. To most people Cyril's truth is far more attractive than the bishop's.

6 March 1995

Threxton church is tiny, with pews for only about 40 people at a squeeze. It nestles by a stream at the bottom of a wooded valley, and is reached by a narrow track; the nearest house – the rambling farmhouse where Cyril and Dot live – is half a mile away. But yesterday afternoon the field nearby was covered with cars. Inside, every corner was filled with members of the five rebel parishes, and with television reporters and newspaper journalists; at the back was a line of cameras.

In theory we were conducting Evensong on the first Sunday in Lent, when the theme is supposed to be the virtues of quietness and simplicity. In practice we were making a profound public statement: that authority over the ministry and management of a church resides – under God – with the people. The television and radio networks and the newspapers are right to take an interest; even the *Sun* sent a reporter, although the sexual angle was obviously her primary focus. Although only a small minority of people attend services every Sunday, a far larger number have a deep spiritual attachment to their local church, and are concerned about the future of religion in this country. So the sight of a bunch of people wresting control of their church from higher authorities is a major news story.

I deliberately, but rather riskily, did not prepare my sermon. I preach best without notes – although sometimes I can preach appallingly. More importantly I wanted to respond to the spirit of the situation. As I arrived one of the journalists told me that the archdeacon had preached that morning in one of the 'conformist' churches, saying that he was engaged in a battle against the forces of Satan. So I was immediately asked, with cameras whirring: 'Do you regard yourself as one of Satan's lieutenants?' Like a true politician I did not answer the question, but spoke instead about the wonderfully loving and Christian spirit amongst the rebels –

and how they are willing at any time to enter into dialogue with the archdeacon.

Astonishingly, once the service began the atmosphere became genuinely devotional; and by the second hymn even some of the journalists were joining in. But I was sharply aware that my sermon was to be the climax of the events: sound bites from it would be shown on television and quoted in newspapers as defining the rebels' position. As I climbed the pulpit I decided to employ the old evangelist's trick – which I use quite frequently anyway – of trying to make people laugh at the beginning, and so ease the tension. Fortunately the trick worked, and I then gave what was almost a lecture on the history of Christianity in Britain, showing that the rebels' stance is true to our ancient traditions. To my amazement – and contrary to normal protocol – both the congregation and the journalists applauded at the end. During the last hymn Cyril Lake, who has been churchwarden at Threxton for almost exactly half a century, took the collection, passing the plate round the reporters as well as the congregation. As he brought the plate up to me at the altar, his eyes twinkled at the sight of so many blue and brown notes – Threxton's largest collection ever.

Afterwards we went to the white and yellow mansion – it looks like a wedding cake – of Philip Jones, the ex-male model, and tucked into a huge spread of cakes. Satan's troops are excellent bakers. Some of the journalists told us that the bishop was going to seek a High Court injunction preventing any further services. Although my knowledge of the law is limited, I can't see how a judge could grant an injunction: the bishop would have to prove that some positive harm was being caused by people worshipping in their local church – and that seems rather improbable. We shall see.

As we drove home we heard extracts of the service and my sermon on the radio news, and later saw the television version. This morning there are large photographs and reports on the front or back pages of most of the papers. Although they purport to be objective, the reports are definitely slanted in our favour. Regardless of whether we are right or wrong, we have a much easier public relations task: David is always more attractive than Goliath.

7 March 1995

In the battle of wills between the rebel parishes and the bishop, the journalists are acting as conduits of information for us. I gather from all three reporters that have telephoned me today that the bishop's lawyers have made tentative moves towards seeking an injunction against us, but have been warned off. Now the bishop's PR officer is cooing about the need for reconciliation. Of course he is right, but I am sceptical. The only basis for reconciliation is for both sides to come together, each side admitting the possibility that it may have made mistakes, and then seeking a common mind. This approach would require the bishop to regard the churchwardens as his equals before God. And while in the privacy of his prayers the bishop may recognize this, the nature of the church as a hierarchy requires him to treat them as subordinates; so reconciliation can only mean submitting to his will. Thus the real problem is a clash of theologies; and, while friendly relations may in the fullness of time be restored, I find it difficult to see the bishop entering a theological debate with the churchwardens.

Some of my economics students were intrigued and astonished to see their lecturer on television in his role as a clergyman. The idea that on Friday a man can be discussing the intricacies of the market mechanism, and then on Sunday preach Christianity 'blows our minds'. As a result the tutorial this afternoon veered off the problem of oligopoly pricing, and, with unanimous consent, went on to religion. (Dutifully I have fixed an extra hour for oligopoly.)

'I thought that to be a Christian you had to belong to a church,' said one young man, 'so what's this business about opting out of the Church?' I replied that to be a Christian meant becoming a disciple of Jesus Christ, and thence joining a community of other disciples; it didn't necessarily mean belonging to a large hierarchical institution. This led quite naturally to the question:

'Why then are you a clergyman in a hierarchical institution?' I answered that originally the parish churches of Britain were a loose-knit federation, and that we were trying to return to this system.

A girl, who bravely declared herself to be a 'practising Roman Catholic' (a label which deters potential boyfriends), raised the question of order: 'If there is no hierarchy, how can you ensure that everyone believes the same doctrines and abides by the same moral principles?' This gets to the theological heart of the dispute. As a system of management hierarchy is notoriously inefficient, and, in modern business practice, is discredited. But bishops and priests ultimately justify their existence as guardians of Christian doctrines and morals; and their underlying assumption is that individuals are 'saved' through believing certain things and abiding by certain rules of behaviour.

In their tolerance towards Kit's marital odyssey, the people of the rebel parishes have shown that in their view Christianity is not about moral rules, but is about the quality of love and forgiveness. The Roman Catholic girl expressed strong disapproval of remarriage after divorce: 'it devalues the whole idea of life-long fidelity'. But most of the other students in the group were impressed that a bunch of old-fashioned farmers in a remote corner of Norfolk would be so open-minded.

The Catholic girl then pressed me on the question of doctrines: 'If these people reject the authority of bishops, they will soon start believing anything they like.'

'And what's wrong with that?' another girl asked. This led to a discussion about whether religion was about accepting things on trust, just because bishops told you, or about exploring the truth. One of the boys in the group announced himself to be a Buddhist. He said that if these farmers in Norfolk were genuine seekers after the truth, he would happily go and pray with them. 'Buddhism teaches that all religions are one.' The Catholic girl protested that this was nonsense, to which the Buddhist rather piously replied: 'Your attitude is the reason why there have been so many wars of religion.' All the others who expressed an opinion were clearly on the side of the Buddhist.

I doubt whether Cyril Lake and company have yet considered whether their attitude to the bishop implies a spiritual openness to other religions!

12 March 1995

A middle-aged man who lives in a hostel for the mentally ill put forward the proposal, framed in words that were admirably direct: 'We want Edie Garvie as our pastor.' There was a brief discussion as to whether a more formal resolution was needed, but happily it was felt that such plain English would suffice. It was seconded by a lady who fosters mentally handicapped children, and passed unanimously.

Then more complex issues arose. How do we make Edie our pastor – is some special service needed? Does some higher authority have to approve Edie – and, if so, which higher authority? The Christian Presence, meeting in a tatty hall in the midst of a run-down Peterborough housing estate, has the grand status of a 'local ecumenical project', which means in theory that all the various denominations – Anglican, Baptist, Methodist, and so on – have some interest in it. Yet does this mean, we asked, that we must seek permission from all these different hierarchies for Edie to be pastor? And if one of them had objections, would that scupper her? The very thought that some remote bishop or moderator could decide our fate generated considerable anger: 'They've never lifted a finger to help us; so what right have they got to poke their fingers in our affairs?'

We were entering deep theological waters, swimming between two different models of the church, and, over our cup of coffee after the Sunday morning service, we were having to choose between the models. Is the church a hierarchy, in which those at the top can choose the leaders of the local congregations? Or is the wider Church simply a federation of local churches, each of which chooses its own leaders? The problem is made even more complex by the schizoid nature of most denominations. At first glance the Church of England looks like a hierarchy, but traditionally parishes have enjoyed considerable autonomy in ministry and management. Conversely, the Methodist Church was at its inception a loosely knit collection of local Methodist 'societies', but it has become highly centralized, with the national body sending ministers to local circuits.

The dominant tendency in the Christian Presence is towards autonomy: they want Edie as their pastor, and nothing will stop them. Yet, like rebellious teenagers, they would still like the approval of the denominations that spawned them. So we decided to hold a service in three months' time at which we will authorize Edie as pastor. We will invite the leaders of all the denominations to attend this service and even to take some role in conducting it. If they accept the invitation, we will interpret that as approval; if they refuse, we will not allow ourselves to feel anxious. The long gap between now and the service will give these leaders ample time to consider their response. In the meantime Edie can began to act as pastor.

In fact, Edie has been pretty active already. Last Christmas she organized a most wonderful service, which I conducted, at the local centre for the mentally handicapped: it was a joyful riot of carols and mince pies. And she is now organizing an Easter sequel, with chocolate eggs instead of mince pies. She has found a young woman to run a Sunday School, which takes place in an adjoining room during the morning service. She is establishing a team to visit the elderly – the members of the team are mostly quite old themselves – and another team of 'helping hands', consisting of unemployed men willing to do odd jobs for the elderly. And she and I are to try and find someone to start working amongst the teenagers on the estate. Edie herself is not especially good at any of the particular jobs required in an active church, but she has an astonishing gift for finding people for each job, and instilling them with enthusiasm. She is very direct – 'Liz, I am convinced you should run a Sunday School' – without being bossy.

Meanwhile, in the Norfolk Saga, the *Church Times* in its leader column has called for me to be defrocked. And their regular writer, Hugh Montefiore, a retired bishop, has accused me of 'fomenting schism'. Happily the Inquisition is now defunct,

28 March 1995

'History is a fable agreed upon.' My main task in the rebel parishes of Breckland is to supply the historical fable on which to base their protest. The bishop and his followers have a different fable, which carries opposite implications.

Our fable is that the historical roots of British Christianity are Celtic, and that we are 'radical' in the true sense of returning to our roots. So our heroes are men like Columba, Aidan, Cuthbert and, as I've just discovered, Fursey, who was the Celtic apostle of Norfolk itself. Yesterday I visited the Roman fort, Burgh Castle, near Great Yarmouth, which Fursey used as his base. It is a most magical place, the size of a football pitch, with high flint and brick walls on three sides, overlooking the Yare estuary on the open side. Fursey arrived there from Ireland in about 630 AD, probably in a small coracle with a sail, and then persuaded some young local men to join him in forming a monastery. Once the young men had fully embraced the gospel, Fursey led them across the county, converting people to Christianity and forming small Christian groups in each village. Many of the churches we see today were probably built on the sites where these groups gathered for worship.

The Celtic Christian literature which survives gives us ample support in our approach to faith, morality and church organization. The Celts sat very lightly on doctrine; for them faith consisted in learning to see God's presence in every creature, and his providence in every event. Thus they wrote the most exquisite poetry celebrating the divine beauty of all natural things. Similarly they sat lightly on moral rules; they believed that good behaviour will occur spontaneously when people see the presence of God in one another – so morality is the outward expression of faith. It follows from these attitudes that large religious institutions, enforcing particular beliefs and rules, are quite unnecessary;

all we need are small local communities of people worshipping together and loving one another, according to Christ's teaching.

The opposite fable honours Augustine of Canterbury as the founder of the English Church. He was sent to Britain by Pope Gregory not merely to spread the gospel, but to bring the existing Celtic Christians under papal control. Bede tells the story of how Augustine invited the Celtic leaders to meet him, and demanded that they recognize him as their bishop. They went away to consider the matter, consulting a wise old hermit as to whether they should submit to Augustine. He advised them that Augustine was only worthy to be their leader if he showed himself to be meek and humble, and the test was whether at their next meeting he rose from his chair to greet them. He remained firmly seated, and they rejected him.

After a further half century of conflict between Celt and Roman the matter was finally settled at the Synod of Whitby in 664. One fable – the fable which we oppose – sees the Synod as an outright victory for the Roman model of church life. Thereafter, the fable goes, a network of dioceses was established, with bishops in firm control. Doctrinal and moral orthodoxy was enforced, and clergy were appointed by the bishops to each parish. The Reformation is regarded as little more than a hiccup in this system of ministry, so the Church of England is regarded as a continuation of the Roman model.

Our fable, however, regards the Synod as an uneasy compromise. Certainly Wilfred, on behalf of the Romans, won over King Oswy, who had convened the meeting and was acting as judge and jury. But his arguments were insulting and fallacious. He accused the Celts of narrow-minded bigotry: 'The only people stupid enough to disagree with the whole world are these Scots, and their obstinate adherents, the Picts and Britons, who inhabit only a tiny portion of these two islands in the ocean.' And then to the Celts' disgust he took the name of Columba and his successors in vain: 'Although your fathers were holy men, do not imagine that they, a small number in the far corner of this remote island, are to be preferred to the universal church throughout the world.' As Wilfred's words revealed, the debate was not about truth or falsehood – numbers of supporters prove nothing in that regard, as the experience of Jesus himself showed – but about asserting control and achieving uniformity, rather than allowing freedom and diversity.

The immediate result of King Oswy's judgment in favour of Rome was that the Celts had to accept a system of dioceses; they also had to alter their way of calculating the date of Easter, and their monks had to adopt a new style of haircut. But in their view the bishops who occupied the diocesan thrones had no authority to control their attitudes and beliefs, still less to manage their churches. Their role was, in the Celtic mind, purely 'apostolic'. Like the first apostles they should travel from place to place, preaching the gospel and inspiring the faithful. In many respects this view of bishops persisted. For over a thousand years local churches retained a high degree of autonomy in organizing their own ministry and material affairs. It was only in the 19th century, when the state began to assert control over social affairs, that the Church of England followed suit, instituting the Ecclesiastical Commissioners to manage a growing proportion of its assets. And as the state has become ever more dominant in secular matters, so the Church of England has created parallel bureaucracies to regulate parishes.

So, to amend Emerson's dictum, 'History is a fable disagreed upon.'

13 April 1995

Immediately before the first rebel service at Threxton, the Bishop of Ely – in whose diocese I live – wrote to me, instructing me not to conduct the service. I replied giving my reasons for going ahead. I mentioned the legal issues: in my view the Bishop of Norwich had been wrong in failing to consult the churchwardens when he licensed Tony Foottit as priest-in-charge; but equally I was breaking canon law in conducting worship in a diocese where I did not have the bishop's permission. But I mainly emphasized Scriptural principle: that Christian ministry of every form requires the consent of those being served. The Bishop of Ely, Stephen Sykes, wrote back to say that he did not accept my arguments, and asked me to come and see him. The afternoon of Maundy Thursday – today – was the only time we could both manage.

I had a sense of being tried as he interrogated me in his study, but as always he spoke with grace and good manners. He began by asking for the Scriptural texts on which I was basing my illegal actions. I replied that my main text is Acts 6 in which the apostles in Jerusalem asked the people to pick their own leaders, and then laid hands on the men chosen. I also quoted 1 Peter 5, and various other passages which strongly suggest that the leaders in the early churches saw themselves as servants of the people and answerable to them; and I also mentioned Jesus' words about leadership as service. I concluded that a grave wrong had been committed in trying to force a priest on unwilling parishes, and I was acting to support them. The bishop responded by quoting Paul's disagreements with the Corinthian church, saying that Paul was trying to impose his will on the people, and was appealing to his own apostolic authority to justify himself. I answered that Paul was offering firm guidance, as a modern bishop may do, but he recognized that power lay in the hands of the local leaders, to whom he refers by name. I think we agreed that consent should be the norm; but he asserted that in extreme cases – as in Corinth then, and perhaps in Breckland now – the bishop must retain final authority.

He then took the conversation on to the need for unity between the bishop and the parishes in his diocese; and he suggested that I was trying to start my own denomination by breaking this unity. I replied that, even if I had such a stupid and wicked intention, the people in Breckland – and in Upton, for that matter – would not follow me. The real point is that these 'rebels' are objecting to the very notion of denomination, in the sense of a large religious institution with a label. The fact that denominations exist causes division; so the logical conclusion of the rebels' action is to bring unity between all Christians. As for the Bishop of Norwich, the rebels would welcome him at any of their services, and gladly listen to him preach the gospel.

Stephen Sykes was visibly exasperated by all this. As he said to me at a previous meeting, he believes that religious institutions are God's vehicles for carrying the truth from one generation to the next; so Christianity without institutions cannot exist. But on this occasion he decided not to pursue this point. Instead he asked me if I would go and see the assistant bishop in Norfolk, David Connor, in the hope of fostering reconciliation. I replied that I was willing to speak to anyone at any time in the cause of Christian unity, and undertook to write to David Connor at once.

In the hallway outside the bishop's study there is a series of portraits of previous bishops, all dressed in their purple regalia. As I walked past them, I remembered the remark a Greek Orthodox priest had made when confronted with a similar array of episcopal portraits: 'Why are there no religious pictures here?'

20 April 1995

Just as comedians say that they feed off their audience, so preachers feed off their congregation; at least, I do. And the congregation in Breckland is extremely nourishing. Actually, in my case, the analogy between comedian and preacher is very close, probably too close, because my instinctive test of whether I am reaching a congregation is whether they laugh at my jokes. Breckland people do with enthusiasm. They are mostly well-educated, so quite sophisticated quips go down well, as do quite subtle theological points. And they like to be gently insulted and goaded; in conversation afterwards, or even occasionally during the sermon itself, they will often return the insults.

Until the rebellion most people only attended their parish church, so, since the villages are tiny, congregations were rarely more than a handful. But now there is a single service each Sunday for all five churches; and the congregation is on average around 50 people. In addition to making the services more jolly and the hymns more lively, it makes it easier for newcomers to have a taste; in a small congregation newcomers feel horribly conspicuous, but in a larger group they disappear in the crowd. The churchwardens tell me that between 10 and 15 of the people now coming to our services have not been attending worship previously.

When I can identify these new worshippers, I seek them out during the coffee and cakes (or tea and cakes in the afternoon) after the service. To my pleasant surprise, some of them describe themselves as 'non-believers', but say that they feel at home in our services. In these cases I have been able to take the conversation deeper, and their reasons are the same. The rebellion excited their interest, because they have always felt alienated by the institutional church – 'it doesn't seem to have anything to do with real Christianity'. Moreover, they feel very heartened by the sight of parishioners sticking by a man in marital difficulties, rather than condemning him. And, having started attending the services, they have been impressed at how open-minded and open-hearted the people seem to be, open-minded in their attitude to religious belief, and open-hearted in their welcome.

One of them said: 'This is the church of the future.' I waved my arm towards the assembled throng supping Earl Grey tea and munching rich fruit cake: 'Are these people, in their tweedy coats and jackets, the Christians of the future?'

'I realize that they don't look very futuristic,' she replied, 'but if I could persuade my teenage son to come along, and really talk to them, I think he might look at religion with fresh eyes.' I asked her how her teenage son might react to the old-fashioned hymns and prayers we use. 'Well, he thinks most of the new pop hymns that he hears are wet – like rather bad seventies music. So he might actually enjoy "Praise my soul" and "Onward Christian Soldiers". He's studying *King Lear* for A-level and says that the poetry is great, so he might think the same about the old *Prayer Book*.'

Sadly, I'm not convinced that today's teenagers will ever flock to sing *Hymns Ancient and Modern* or to recite Cranmer's liturgy. I belong to the last generation that was brought up with those tunes and words, so in middle and old age we find them wonderfully resonant and reassuring, but that won't apply to today's generation. On the other hand they can hear the gospel with much fresher and less prejudiced ears than we did. The lady with the teenage son is quite right to think that while the gospel is identified with mighty institutions it will remain inaudible to the next generation. But these tweedy cake-munchers have understood the gospel and can speak about it in a way that young people could begin to hear and grasp.

This church may be the church of the future if their rebellion succeeds, and if others follow their lead.

26 April 1995

'Jesus Christ was the supreme salesman. Of course, he had a wonderful product: eternal salvation through loving God and loving your neighbours. However, lots of others have tried to sell similar products with little success, but Jesus is still being talked about two thousand years after his sales campaign.' That is roughly what John O'Dwyer, one of the Oxborough churchwardens, and his wife Valerie said to me over tea and cakes the other day. They are both professional salespeople – he markets British cakes across the world, and she organizes the advertising and public relations for four large hotels – and one of their grown-up daughters is also a marketing whizkid. There was, however, a sting in the tail in their eulogy of Jesus Christ's sales technique: 'Nowadays the church seems to have lost the knack of selling Christianity. Congregations are falling steadily – two or three per cent a year according to the statistics – so we're not getting the message through. What can we do?'

The context of the discussion was the prospect of no longer having a priest presiding over their church's affairs. Until now the task of selling Christianity has rested on the shoulders of the vicar; and, while they may have grumbled at the shortcomings of the clergy, they have not felt responsible. But now they have committed themselves to managing their own affairs, the burden rests on them – and, as they emphasized, on the congregation as a whole. 'And that is exactly how it should be.' So what should happen?

Looking at Christianity through their marketing eyes yields some fascinating insights. First of all: 'The pattern of the week is changing, with Sunday becoming like Saturday used to be. So we should consider moving our main acts of worship away from Sunday.' They pointed out that most leisure activities experience peak demand on Sunday, it's the busiest day for sport, and many shops are now open on Sunday. Moreover, since most women go out to work, families have to do all the household chores at the weekends. 'So why not put on services on weekday evenings from time to time – when most social clubs and organizations now meet?' And they pointed out that Jesus was 'pretty relaxed' about the notion of a Sabbath day.

Secondly: 'Why do we have to meet for public worship every week? Perhaps it is just too often for most people nowadays; their lives are too busy. Much better to have a few popular services, than many unpopular ones – a full, lively church is a much better advertisement for the Christian faith.' So what would be a good starting point? 'Let's make better use of the festivals. If each service had a different flavour – a different focus – it would help to sustain interest.' This led to an immediate application of the market approach: 'Next Sunday is St George's Day; let's make the service a St George festival.' And that is exactly what happened a couple of days ago. Valerie bought 50 little plastic flags with St George's red cross, and pinned little posters advertising the service on trees and posts throughout the village. And I prepared a suitable talk, and played jolly patriotic hymns on my guitar. The church was packed.

As a part-time businessman, I share the assumption which lies behind John and Valerie's approach, that 'the customer is always right'. As a clergyman, my training (such as it was) taught me to regard the church as always right; and while we might make some concessions to make the church more attractive, the clear message is that people must fit firmly within the church's framework. So to apply the values of marketing so forcefully to worship itself is quite disturbing – and challenging.

My instinct is that John and Valerie are essentially right. The present routine of services each Sunday, following the same format week by week, is a burden which the great majority of people can't or won't bear; hence the falling congregations. And at the current rate of decline, which has been continuous over several decades, most parish churches will cease to exist in a generation or two. And festival services are undoubtedly popular: again, according to statistics, attendance at carol services is actually increasing across the nation as a whole. Of course, it would be wonderful if people prayed more on their own or in small groups; and the corollary of the O'Dwyers' approach is that people may need help in learning to do this. The issue which they are raising is the public face of the church: it looks distinctly gloomy at present, and they want to put a smile on it.

For most priests the leap which John and Valerie propose is virtually impossible. Only when the laity are in charge, bringing insights from outside, does it seem not only possible, but vital.

30 April 1995

'The government aeroplanes dropped bombs near our village and then shells began to land on us. Thirty men, women and children were killed, and the church, along with many homes, was destroyed. I led the people southwards out of the village and across the border into Uganda. Now we are waiting at a collection centre near the Nile River, and we will soon be told where to go.' This is the second paragraph of a letter we have just received from Sam Kokini. The first paragraph reads: 'Welcome, brother and sister, in the name of the Lord Jesus. May his joy and peace be upon you. We pray every day for you, giving thanks for your love for us. And we thank God for all the blessings he pours on us.'

In the third paragraph he expresses the hope that the United Nations authorities, who are looking after the refugees from Sudan, will send them to a place where they can rebuild their village – for the second time in five years. 'As soon as we have shelter where we can sleep, we will build another church. Even in our present situation we have so many reasons to praise God. Above all, we have the joy of Jesus Christ in our hearts. So always our first priority is to honour God and to worship Him.'

Their appalling situation puts our own problems in Breckland into perspective; and their capacity to thank God makes our faith seem puny. My immediate reaction is to want to catch the first plane back to East Africa, and then make the tortuous journey up to northern Uganda to be with Sam and his people. There we would be fighting a real battle for Christ, whereas here it seems like shadow-boxing. I visited that refugee collection centre, and the image of those crowds of people sitting forlornly on the parched, dusty earth, their eyes empty with despair and their bodies weak with hunger, is etched in my memory. If I was with them, I could be negotiating with officials to get them a piece of fertile land where they could build their huts and plant their crops.

But by now their destiny will have been decided. Perhaps they have been forced to break up into small groups, and been allocated to different refugee camps. Or perhaps they have been allowed to stay together, and been given their own little area in which to create a new life. In either case they will be dependent on the United Nations for the next few months; and they will only be able to grow their own food if their land is fertile. So my presence would just be another mouth to feed. And even donations of money are now useless, since they will not be permitted to travel and buy things. In effect, they are now prisoners until the southern Sudan is peaceful enough for them to return.

Yet I know that once Sam and his people are settled, their joy in Christ will bubble up again. I attended services in refugee camps where people were dying daily of cholera, and yet the smiles on the worshippers' faces were as broad as their faces would allow. So in spirit Sam's people will continue to put all our comfortable little congregations in Britain to shame.

If our battle in Breckland and in Upton and Hamerton is just about power over a few village churches, then we should give up immediately. Sam and his people have proved utterly powerless in the face of the Sudanese army, and yet their faith is stronger than ever. To be honest, power *is* one of the issues here, and there is some satisfaction in cutting bishops and archdeacons down to size; yet somehow we must push all thoughts of power, and all pleasure in gaining power, out of our minds and hearts.

Only if our battle is about the gospel is the battle worth fighting. At heart I believe it is. In their own buttoned-up way, our people look at their church made of stone with the same eyes that Sam's people look at their bamboo church: as the home of God's family in their village, and thus as a sign of God's presence in their midst. So both our people and Sam's people take more pride in their church than in their private homes. More importantly, our people are as eager to serve one another as Sam's people; and Sam's people chose him as pastor in order to lead them in their mutual ministry. That is the kind of pastor which our people want. In the present crisis Sam and his congregation have reached out to their whole village, leading them to safety; so in the comfort of rural

England our congregations are looking for ways to reach out to their villages. Outwardly our circumstances could hardly be more different; but inwardly the spiritual vision is the same.

5 May 1995

For the week's tutorials in my university course on 'Methods of Management' I had told my students to read 1 Corinthians 12 and Romans 12, and then write a brief paper on Paul's style of management. When I gave these references at the end of last week's tutorial it took some time to explain what they meant. Most students had never heard of Paul, had no idea that he wrote letters, and didn't know how to find a copy of the New Testament. After initial resistance I agreed to photocopy the relevant passages.

But despite their ignorance of the Bible, the students' reactions were just as I had hoped.

'Paul was the pioneer of the flat organization.'

'Paul organized his churches just like Hewlett-Packard organize their headquarters.'

'The Corinthian Church was managed just like a modern high-tech firm.'

'Why has modern industry only just woken up to the idea of the flat organization when Paul knew about it two thousand years ago?'

The Hewlett-Packard HQ is apparently organized around a large covered garden, with lots of individual offices – or 'work stations' – leading on to it. The role of the managers is to work out all the specific tasks required for each project, and then allocate those tasks to individuals. People are encouraged to emerge from time to time from their work stations into the garden and to chat to colleagues, discussing problems and bouncing ideas off one another; and they are free to choose to whom they talk. This system is proving hugely successful, and in varying degrees is being adopted throughout the commercial and industrial world. Instead of hierarchies, in which reports are pushed upwards and orders pushed downwards, everyone is equal; and the role of manager is to assure that the gifts and skills of each individual are used to the maximum advantage of the firm as a whole.

And this, of course, is exactly how Paul ran his churches. They were the original flat organizations, with individuals contributing to the whole according to their various gifts and skills – as preachers, teachers, healers, evangelists, counsellors, administrators, and so on. The pastors or elders in the first churches were like the managers at Hewlett-Packard, discerning and coordinating these gifts. And just as Hewlett-Packard bursts with intellectual energy, Paul's community burst with spiritual energy – and attracted new adherents at an astonishing rate.

Yet the one type of organization today that remains virtually untouched by the revolution in management is the church. Despite having invented the flat organization the institutional churches remain rigidly hierarchical. As one student, who belongs to an Anglican church, put it: 'Why doesn't the church practise what it preaches?' In the industrial world firms organized like the institutional church have long ago been forced either to adapt or to die; either they have cut drastically their layers of management or they have gone bust. The institutional church, by contrast, has remained arrogantly indifferent to the problems of industry, imagining that its hierarchical structure has been ordained by God.

But the institutional church, it seems to me, is now heading towards some kind of spiritual bankruptcy. Like the industrial firms which refused to adapt, its products – the kind of faith and worship it offers – seem dull and shabby, so sales – bottoms on pews – continue to fall. And like the industrial dinosaurs, its salary bill remains obstinately high; so worshippers must pay more and more for less and less.

'If the church you belong to is so badly organized, why don't you start a new one on good management principles? After all, Paul started his own churches.' I paused for a moment, 'The church,' I replied, 'is like a supermarket chain with masses of branches. The most sensible strategy is to improve how the existing branches operate, rather than tear them down and build afresh.'

16 May 1995

Castle Acre, a few miles north of Swaffham, was the site of a huge Cluniac abbey. Today, the great church and cloister have been reduced to a few flint pillars rising up from the grass. But the abbot's house has remained virtually intact, and even by modern standards it is spacious and comfortable, with large open fires in every room. Overlooking the abbey ruins is an even more spacious and comfortable house: the Edwardian rectory, which has become the official residence of the Bishop of Lynn, David Conner, assistant to the Bishop of Norwich.

As my rusty – and remarkably trusty – car, with almost a quarter of a million miles on the clock, scrunched up the gravel drive, I could see through the study window the bishop and the archdeacon in earnest conversation. The bishop looked out, but then turned away; and when I rang the door-bell I had to wait at least a minute, while through the study window I could see these two senior clergy finishing their conversation. No doubt Peter Nott would have received a more vigorous welcome, but then the Church of England is riddled with little games of etiquette and dress, designed to put people in their place. I, too, was playing a game by arriving slightly late and wearing jeans and an open-necked shirt.

The sense of game-playing continued once I was let into the house. I was put in a very low armchair, while the bishop and archdeacon were both in high Windsor chairs. As the bishop's wife brought us coffee and biscuits, the three of us engaged in rather awkward banter, mainly about mutual clerical acquaintances. After about five minutes, the bishop put his coffee cup loudly down on the table, cleared his throat, and said: 'So we ought to discuss the rebellion.' Then he turned to me: 'My main purpose this morning is to hear your views and insights.'

By all accounts this bishop is an extremely shrewd operator; if so, he was using a ploy – which I too sometimes use – that seems generous and respectful, but actually pushes the other person into a corner. I now had to state clearly my position before I had heard his. I decided to play straight. I put, in very bold and unequivocal terms, precisely why, in my view, the Bishop of Norwich had acted both against Scripture and against the law, and why the Breckland people were showing remarkable Christian love and under-standing in their actions. To my surprise, both the bishop and archdeacon were startled by what I said. As they admitted – and later tried to retract – they had never before heard the points I was expressing, because Peter Nott had not shown them the letters which the Breckland people had written. Indeed, I sensed that David Conner was rather peeved at being so badly briefed by his boss.

He now changed tack completely. 'I believe that we bishops often confuse authority with power.'

'Could you expand?'

'We think our job is about exercising power, giving orders and telling people what to do. But it is about authority: the church has given us spiritual authority to act as guides, enabling local parishes to fulfil their potential.'

'Does this mean you will not try to force a new priest on these parishes against their will?'

'What I am saying is that it is not a bishop's job to use force. And I would ask you to carry that message back to the rebel parishes.'

I agree wholly with his theology, and I said so; indeed, it is what I have been saying from the pulpit, and on television and radio. So were his words offered as an olive branch, a gesture of reconcilia-tion, inviting the churchwardens through me back into friendly dialogue? Or was he pronouncing a threat, that while he would prefer not to exert power, he may try to do so if his spiritual authority is defied? We shall see.

11 June 1995

The archdeacon, Tony Foottit, has circulated a letter to every house in the five rebel parishes to say that he, and he alone, is the only person legally entitled to conduct baptisms, weddings and funerals in their churches, and that any such services arranged by the rebel churchwardens are thereby illegal. In fact, a wedding had already been arranged in Oxborough, and I had been invited to conduct it; and the day after the archdeacon's letter dropped through the villagers' letterboxes, one of the oldest inhabitants of Oxborough died.

The death provoked an unseemly scramble. Kit knew the family well, and had been visiting the old man through his final illness. So, naturally, as soon as he heard that the old man had died, he drove over to the house to comfort the family. They asked him to organize the funeral in Oxborough church, followed by burial in the churchyard. The following day the archdeacon arrived, and told the family that they could only have a funeral in church if he conducted it; otherwise they would have to go to King's Lynn crematorium 30 miles away. The family were extremely upset. 'Members of our family have always been buried in the churchyard; and we want Kit to arrange it. Why can't we have what we want at a time like this?' The archdeacon was unmoved.

Kit telephoned me for advice. I am quite sure that the archdeacon's legal arguments are nonsensical, and told Kit that since the archdeacon has not been legally licensed to the five rebel parishes, the churchwardens have responsibility for arranging baptisms, weddings and funerals. If they are happy to delegate this to him, that is their affair. But Kit remained extremely reluctant to conduct any services, for fear of further wrath from the bishop. He asked me to take the funeral, if he organized it. He did a superb job. The old man had been an ardent racegoer, and in his youth had been a stable lad. So Kit managed to find a splendid black horse, ridden by his owner in a magnificent green and gold jacket, to lead the hearse through the village to the church. The family's gratitude was boundless; it is just the kind of touch that has made Kit so popular.

But after the service one of the churchwardens at Oxborough, the retired Home Service announcer, told me that his wife had died that morning. So immediately Kit had to organize another funeral. And, since she and Kit had been very close, Kit wanted to give the address – but was full of anxieties about doing so. Right up to the funeral itself Kit was dithering, so I prepared an address in case his courage failed. But at the vital moment he rose from his pew, his entire body trembling, and climbed gingerly up into the pulpit. During the first few sentences his voice kept cracking; then he gave a loud cough, and his words became firm and clear. He is not a natural preacher, but once his body stopped shaking he exuded great warmth and love.

And today I conducted the wedding: a middle-aged couple who have recently moved into the village.

It seems wrong to think of these events as anything other than religious ceremonies. Yet they marked a major psychological victory for the rebel parishes. About half the population of most villages attends church at least once a year for a festival service, but virtually everyone comes occasionally for weddings and funerals. The archdeacon rightly spotted that if the rebel churches could be prevented from holding weddings and funerals, they would sooner or later lose the support of the local people. But by organizing two funerals and a wedding – and especially a funeral procession which the entire village came out to see – the rebels have discredited the archdeacon and won the locals over to their side. Moreover, Kit's self-confidence, so horribly battered, is now immeasurably strengthened.

23 June 1995

Susie and I are close rivals in indiscretion: she talks almost continuously, so secrets flow out with the harmless gossip, and I am
unable to distinguish secrets from the normal run of information.
But both of us managed to keep our mouths shut about her marriage to Kit; otherwise we would have been besieged with television cameras and microphones.

Apart from Kit and Susie's respective children, all of whom are
grown-up and seven of them married, and Kit's 89-year-old parents, the guest list was confined to the rebel churchwardens and
their spouses. So when the guests arrived in the church there was
a conspiratorial atmosphere. But that soon dissolved as five grandchildren, dressed as bridesmaids and page boys, quarrelled loudly
in the porch over their positions behind the bride. Finally, the
marching order was agreed, and I led the procession towards the
altar. Music was provided by an old friend of Kit's playing the
accordion – which had the effect of making me want to giggle.
Susie spent much of the service fussing over the grandchildren
but managed to concentrate for the vows themselves. Afterwards
there was a huge spread of food, entirely prepared by Susie; she
cultivates an air of scattiness, but she is military in her domestic
arrangements.

During the service I had the unworthy thought: 'What if the
marriage doesn't work, and Kit and Susie split up? The rest of us
will look utter fools.' The truth is that, for our various reasons, the
churchwardens and I have staked a great deal on Kit and Susie's
future happiness. Initially last Christmas the churchwardens were
simply incensed at Kit's summary dismissal, and wanted to find
some way of hanging on to him; only gradually have they come to
see the wider implications of their actions. I by contrast did not
know Kit, but in the light of our experience in Upton and
Hamerton, I could see the wider implications at once.

Either way Kit and Susie are at the heart of the rebellion, and remain its symbol. The churchwardens are standing against a hierarchy which attempts to rule congregations without consent, and they are standing up for the right of congregations to choose their own pastor. In simple terms it is a battle for ecclesiastical freedom. But the churchwardens are also standing against the notion that morality is a set of rules – rules which Kit has transgressed – and standing up for moral freedom, rooted in forgiveness and love. In principle their stance would still be right even if tomorrow Kit and Susie had the most terrible row, and went their separate ways. But those who believe that bishops know best, and that strict moral rules are our only protection against emotional chaos, would be able to wag their fingers gleefully, and say, 'We told you so'.

Kit must now decide his future ministry. The Bishop of Norwich has put his name on something called the Lambeth List, which appears to be the ultimate clerical disgrace: the other names include convicted paedophiles and embezzlers of church funds. So, to use the old-fashioned term, he has been 'defrocked', and is unlikely ever again to be 'refrocked'. Kit's first reaction to being told this was bitter humiliation and despair: 'I am like an artist whose brushes have been taken away.' But despair is now turning into a burning sense of injustice, which is giving him courage. Already he is visiting parishioners in the rebel villages, and some in the other villages, on two or three days each week.

The next stage is for him to overcome his anxieties about conducting worship. The churchwardens realize that I cannot continue indefinitely travelling 80 miles to their parishes every time Communion is celebrated, and want Kit to resume before the winter, so they are dropping heavy hints. I sense that Kit feels that one day he will take up the liturgical reins again, but after a lifetime of loyal service to the Church of England he can't yet bring himself to break the rules.

Strangely, my feelings are rather similar to Kit's. The logic of the situation is that sooner or later Kit will again be pastor of the five parishes. This is manifestly what people want, and Kit is manifestly an excellent pastor. But, as someone who has spent half a lifetime as a loyal servant of the Church of England, I am fearful of the consequences. At present the churchwardens can justly claim to be acting legally, and I alone am outside the law by conducting worship without the bishop's permission. But if they ask Kit, as someone whom the bishop has defrocked, to lead services, and Kit accepts . . .

26 June 1995

I had imagined that when we started our building firm, offering to repair churches at half the normal cost, churchwardens would flock to us: the thought of having to arrange fewer garden fêtes and jumble sales in order to mend the roof or repoint the walls would overcome any inhibitions. But I had underestimated the tenacity of the architects. They took one look at our brochure and realized that halving the cost of building work would mean their fees would also be cut in half. So, as various churchwardens have told me, church architects, without evidence, described us as 'cowboys' and said that they could take 'no responsibility for the consequences' if we were employed.

I had also underestimated the unwillingness which most church people have of defying those in authority. Parishes must appoint architects from a list approved by the diocese, so to resist their advice feels like an act of revolt. From Monday to Friday many churchwardens are business people and are quite ruthless about cutting costs, even if it means sacking people. But on Sunday they become passively compliant, preferring to pay ludicrously high prices for church repairs than to risk causing offence to those set above them.

Yet astonishingly one of the architects has changed sides. He recently took on an idealistic young assistant who is more dedicated to keeping churches watertight than filling his own pocket. I met this young man at a conference last April, and persuaded him that, if he and his boss were shrewd, idealism and profit could go hand in hand: that by working with us in halving the costs of repairs, they would quickly gain a high reputation, and churchwardens would appoint them. He then persuaded his boss of the wisdom of this approach, and they are now eagerly employing us. As I predicted, eight churches have already dismissed their existing architects, and turned to these architects instead – and the trend will surely continue.

The churchwardens in those eight churches seem wonderfully elated at what they have done. They have all told me that they long suspected price-rigging in church repairs, but felt it was impossible for an individual parish to break the system. But now the system is being broken from within, and they are delighted to be playing a part. As one churchwarden put it: 'I feel like a schoolboy who has found a way to make a cruel headmaster look a fool.'

I feel both pleased and disappointed: pleased that at least our efforts are being rewarded, but disappointed that it required someone in authority – an architect approved by the diocese – to allow the churchwardens to defy the system. If the churchwardens knew that prices were being rigged, why didn't they simply ignore the system and make their own arrangements for repairs? The simple answer is that it was psychologically impossible. When the churchwarden spoke of himself as a schoolboy, he was describing precisely the attitude most churchgoers have to those in authority; and most schoolboys want to keep the rules and stay out of trouble.

This is why our little victory in this corner of the county will not spread rapidly elsewhere. And it is also why the rebellion in Breckland will not suddenly set the Church of England alight. Yet there is one force that is even more powerful than the psychology of hierarchy: money. The hierarchy has maintained its hold on people's minds to a great degree because its hands have been on the purse strings, paying the clergy from its vast accumulated assets. Thus parish churches have felt dependent on the hierarchy. But as the assets dwindle, and as parishes are forced to become financially independent again, the hierarchy's grasp on their minds will weaken.

Already many parishes are delaying vital repairs in order to pay the diocesan quota, which is used for clergy salaries. As their churches look increasingly shabby, and the leaks grow worse, they will feel compelled to arrange their own repairs. And as one church after another opts out of the system, so the system itself will weaken and crumble. As for churches making their own pastoral arrangements, like Breckland and Upton and Hamerton, the best hope is for a diocese actually to go bust; there are strong rumours that Edmundsbury (Suffolk) and Truro (Cornwall) are having 'severe cash flow problems'. Most dioceses have already used up their financial reserves. So it would only require a few churches to default on their quota for a diocese no longer to have enough money to meet the salary bill. Once that happens parishes will soon realize that their best hope of retaining a vicar is to pay him or her directly. And once that happens the Breckland rebellion – and the theology which goes with it – becomes the norm.

1 July 1995

'You've lost weight.'

'Thank you for noticing. It is because I'm happy.'

A hundred years or more ago it would have been an insult to accuse someone of losing weight – a smaller tummy was a sign of either poverty or illness. And putting on weight was a sign of contentment. But Richard Titford, my vicar friend from west Suffolk, is happy because he is receiving only half a salary, instead of a whole salary, from his diocese. And instead of constantly nibbling to comfort himself, he now just eats at meal-times.

We met at the radio studio in Cambridge where I had just finished my weekly broadcast, and we walked up to Tatties for coffee and baked potatoes. 'I feel so much younger,' he pronounced as we sat at a scrubbed pine table, 'almost like a student again.' The secret of his restored youth is that he is freeing himself from the shackles of the church. Having for many years been a full-time vicar, obliged to manage the material, as well as spiritual, affairs of three rural parishes, and to sit on several diocesan committees, he has succeeded in becoming half-time. So he no longer has to attend committee meetings, and the churchwardens have agreed to take over the material affairs of the parishes; Richard is required to concentrate solely on pastoral work. And everyone is pleased: the diocesan salary bill has been cut; the amount the parishes had to raise each year has been cut; and Richard has felt a burden fall from his shoulders. In fact, the parishes are so pleased that they continue to pay Richard £3,000 each year for expenses. Richard has made up the shortfall in his income by various part-time activities, including work for our building firm.

Richard and his parishes have now begun to discuss a further development. Like Kit in Norfolk, Richard is a superb pastor, knocking on doors and chatting to people, and he loves doing it. His parishes have decided they want him to do more pastoral work

– 'villaging' as Richard calls it, quoting Francis Kilvert. And he is so popular that people are happy to contribute more money to pay for his time. If he went back on to a full diocesan salary, he could be obliged to sit on all the committees again.

So he and the churchwardens are wondering whether he should come off the diocesan pay-roll altogether, and for their parish quota to be cut by an even greater amount, and for the parishes to pay him directly. There are no legal impediments to this arrangement. And the diocese has no reason to oppose it, since their salary bill will be reduced even further. To the churchwardens, and to Richard himself, it just seems like common sense.

And, of course, it is just common sense. Yet here in a quiet, peaceful way the same revolution is occurring that has caused such a storm in Upton, Hamerton and Breckland. With everyone's approval, a group of rural parishes in Suffolk is breaking away from the financial bureaucracy of their diocese and employing their own pastor.

'One of the things that has impressed me about your rebel parishes,' Richard declared, 'is that, having opted out of the financial system, they are eager to support poorer parishes in the inner cities. I hope our parishes will do the same.'

'My guess is that they will want to,' I replied, 'because once they are free from the system, and have control over their own funds, they will naturally give more money to the church. And they will have ample resources to help other parishes in need.'

'It will be a real test of their faith,' concluded Richard.

Indeed it will. The financial arrangements are common sense, but whether or not they are truly Christian depends on the degree to which people are spurred to greater generosity.

4 July 1995

When the bishop's secretary opened the front door, I could sense she was edgy. 'Ah, Mr Van de Weyer, thank you for coming,' she said without a smile.

'It's my pleasure,' I replied grinning, which provoked her lips to twitch awkwardly.

The Bishop of Ely had been working himself up into a lather of indignation against me, and his secretary feared the outcome. She led me silently up the stairs to the waiting-room, and then disappeared into her office. A few moments later the bishop flung open his study door, and almost shouted at me: 'Come in.'

There was none of the normal small talk. 'I have to tell you, Robert, that your relationship with the Church of England is extremely unstable.'

'Why?'

'Because you are continuing to conduct services in the rebel parishes in Norfolk, and you are making no effort to bring reconciliation between those parishes and the Bishop of Norwich.'

'How do you know I'm making no effort?'

'Because the bishop tells me so.'

'But I've indicated to the bishop that I am willing to talk to him at any time to help mutual understanding, and then act as a go-between.'

'It's not a question of mutual understanding, it's a question of the parishes accepting the bishop's authority – his spiritual and pastoral authority.'

The bishop now changed tack. 'I am quite convinced that the parishes are acting illegally in rejecting Archdeacon Foottit as their priest-in-charge.'

'Why are you convinced of this?'

'Because the Bishop of Norwich has explained to me his legal position.'

'Would it be helpful if I were to explain the parishes' legal position?'

'If you wish.'

I took from my briefcase a fat volume containing all the parliamentary statutes applying to the Church of England, and read out the relevant passages, explaining how they applied to this case.

When I had finished the bishop made no response, but sat in silence, his chin resting on his chest. Finally he lifted his head. 'Robert, I want to say something very important to you.' A further period of silence followed, as he held his tall bald forehead in his thumb and little finger. He then spoke slowly and deliberately: 'There is a long history of people rebelling against the authority of the established Church. Their rebellions almost always come to nothing. In the light of this, there must be a presumption that those in authority, the bishops, are generally right.'

'There is a long history,' I replied, 'of bishops trying to stamp out genuine movements of the Spirit. These movements help to bring the churches back to the simplicity of the gospel. Instead of trying to stamp them out, a wise bishop should listen to what the Spirit is saying through them.'

He sat back in his chair, and tried to smile. 'How is your wife getting on with her training course, and how are your children progressing?' he inquired. The small talk which normally occurs at the start of an episcopal interview was now his means of indicating that the interview was over. I gave a brief sketch of the current state of my family. Then he rose; I put the book of ecclesiastical law back in my case, and rose too. 'Thank you so much for coming over. I'm most grateful. I'm sure you can find your own way out.' And he ushered me through his study door, and closed it firmly – with a slight slam, I think.

So what happened? Was he giving me a warning? Was he saying that if the present situation persists he will defrock me? Or was he metaphorically throwing up his hands in despair at me?

6 July 1995

My perverse nature prompts me to join seemingly inappropriate organizations. Some years ago I signed up to the Lesbian and Gay Christian Movement as an act of solidarity with its cause; and in its membership list a special heterosexual section was started in which to put my name. I eventually resigned over the issue of gay marriages. I believe that gay people should live within the same moral framework as 'straights'; but too many gay Christians talk about their need for 'variety' – which is a euphemism for promiscuity. Since then the AIDS epidemic has curtailed their behaviour, but the Movement remains ambiguous in its moral stance.

At roughly the same time I joined the Mothers' Union. I am not the only male member, but men are certainly a rarity. Despite the very different images of the two organizations, my reasons for joining both were similar: the belief that life-long partnerships – whether gay or straight – are natural and right for the human species. And this moral conviction needs defending at present, so I am proud to belong to any organization which stands up for it.

This afternoon I made a pilgrimage to the place where the Mothers' Union was founded, Old Alresford, near Winchester. I had a meeting in New Alresford – which is a beautiful 18th-century town with a medieval church – and so felt impelled to make a detour. The names are as perverse as my nature: the church in Old Alresford is Victorian, built in the 1850s by the Reverend George Sumner. His wife Mary started the first branch of the Mothers' Union in their vicarage; and the idea spread rapidly across Britain, and then across the world. The church itself is very dull – a long narrow barn with minimal decoration – but a small side chapel has been converted into a shrine to the great woman.

It is dominated by a large photograph of Mary Sumner, dressed in black like the ageing Queen Victoria. There is also a blown-up facsimile of the original membership card, listing the various promises that women made on joining. These included kneeling down with their children every night for prayers, and not giving their children 'wine, spirits, beer or any other strong drink except under doctor's orders'. The Mothers' Union loves to process and there are photographs of two processions, one taken in 1906 and the other in 1986. The women in Edwardian times were much more wrinkled whereas today they are much stouter – a tribute to the excellent cakes served after most branch meetings.

The altar of this side chapel is a wooden shelf underneath the east window, with an open Bible and two candlesticks on it. Below the shelf is a yellow curtain. 'What is behind the curtain, what holy object is kept there to symbolize the Mothers' Union?' I wondered. I gingerly drew back the curtain, half-expecting to find some relic of Mary Sumner, such as a toenail or lock of hair. To my delight there was a large aluminium kettle, and piles of cups and saucers.

Yes, truly a fitting symbol, not just of the Mothers' Union, but of parish churches throughout the country and probably throughout the world. In the time of Jesus wine and bread were the equivalent of tea and cake. And in truth church life at the local level revolves round tea and cake: after services; at social and study meetings; when the vicar comes to call; and whenever two or three Christians gather together for a chat. That's why I remain part of the church. Yes, my relationship with the Church of England is rather unstable, as the bishop says, but that is only at the institutional level. At the parish level I remain passionately in love with the church: I love the tea and cake, and all the events which they mark.

I think the bishop, in a roundabout way, is telling me to consider my position: either I resign from the priesthood and the Church of England; or I become a loyal servant of the institution. But to me this a false choice. The Church of England is not distinct from its parish churches, standing over and above them; it *is* its parish churches. In the past, when each parish enjoyed a high degree of material and spiritual autonomy, this was clear. But even now, when finances have been centralized and clergy deployed from diocesan headquarters, the Church of England remains no more than the sum of its parishes; without the parish churches, it is nothing. My loyalty and devotion to the parishes is as stable as my loyalty and devotion to Sarah, my wife.

Why not change the name from the 'Church *of* England' to the 'Church *in* England'? Anyone who is a Christian and who happens to live in England can claim membership of the Church in England. Thus the notion of the Church in England embraces all brands and varieties – Baptist, Congregationalist, Methodist, Pentecostal and so on, as well as Anglican. Seen in this light the institutional structures wither in importance. Indeed, if you take that line of thinking to its logical conclusion, the central institution becomes rather like the Mothers' Union. A women's group in Upton, Hamerton, Oxborough and such places may choose to affiliate with the MU because of the benefits which such a national and international body can bring, and pay its subscription accordingly; or it may affiliate with another similar body; or it may remain entirely independent. What if the Diocese of Norwich, the RC Diocese of East Anglia, the Methodist District and so on all became voluntary bodies to which local congregations could choose to affiliate? There would be some friendly rivalry, which would induce them to sharpen their acts and give better value for money. But there would also be unity, because all would automatically be part of the Church in England.

I am a Christian, and, despite my foreign name, I am a true-born Englishman. The churches in England, held together with tea and cakes, are my spiritual home. I refuse to be made homeless.

8 July 1995

In organizing a flower festival the first task is to determine the theme. After four consecutive years of flower festivals at Upton, I've concluded that you can pick virtually any theme, and people will adapt their flower-arranging skills to it. In future years we might try 'sewerage' or 'post-modernism' and see what people achieve. But this year, the 50th anniversary of the Allied victory in the Second World War, the church council decided that the theme must reflect this event. 'But we should not celebrate military victory,' said Cecil Dellar, who fought at the Battle of Arnhem, 'because one army's victory is another army's defeat. Those German lads whom we fought were just like us.'

'So what do we celebrate?' asked Mike Newton. A long pause.

'Freedom is what we celebrate,' declared Cecil, 'the Second World War was a victory of freedom over tyranny.' And so it was decided that this year's theme should be freedom.

In a village of barely two hundred people, a dozen prove to be adept flower-arrangers. So this weekend every corner and windowsill of Upton church has been filled with displays. Freedom of speech was illustrated by flowers in the shape of a human face, with its mouth open. Political freedom was a ballot-box borrowed from the district council decked with poppies. Then there was the freedom of wild birds and animals, illustrated by a miniature forest filled with plastic toy creatures. There was even hippy freedom with various memorabilia from the 1960s nestling amidst white lilies.

On the altar was the freedom of Upton church. In the centre was a small wooden model of the church, surrounded by model men and women. Each person had a label signifying his or her spiritual ministry: pastor, teacher, visitor, administrator and encourager. They were standing in the graveyard, with grey cards representing headstones; and on each headstone was written a name, and then a record of the work they had done for the church. Just as in reality the church stands in the centre of the village, looking over the main street, so a model street went from one end of the altar to the other, with doll's houses on either side. And surrounding the whole village was a rainbow, made of coloured paper, to illustrate God's love for everyone. On either side of the altar stood the churchwarden's staves which are the symbol of their office, conferred on them when they are elected by the parishioners.

Upton is now at ease with its freedom. The display was a public statement of that freedom, but not a strident assertion of it; stridency is no longer needed. In fact, 16 months after the people of Upton declared that they would manage their own church, it is as if this has always been the case. No one is complaining of the lack of a proper vicar; no one is anxious that the church and her ministry is in some sense adrift without episcopal oversight. One sign of this normality is that people have gone back to squabbling over the mundane issues, such as whether geese from a nearby farm should be allowed to graze in the churchyard, or whether Mrs Hollis can put plastic flowers on her husband's grave. These quarrels were put aside for a few months when Upton staged her revolution and the television crews rolled into the village. But now that seems like a distant memory, and traditional parish politics have resumed.

Actually, something *has* changed. These politics are more passionate, because people once again feel they own the church. During the 11 years that I was 'priest-in-charge' of Upton, people frequently appealed to me to intervene in some dispute on their side. Now they can no longer turn to me, since I have no power, so they have to sort it out amongst themselves. Far from deterring people from the church, it has drawn more people in. One sign of this is the current debate over the old harmonium, which has been rotting in a corner for as long as anyone can remember. In April the church council finally decided to get rid of it, selling the case to the highest bidder. In the past no one outside the council would have reacted, because they assumed that the vicar, as chairman of the council, had absolute power. But now a group has formed within the village, who have asked the council to delay implementing their decision, and are now busily raising money to restore the instrument.

So an audit on the Upton revolution could be expressed quite simply: attendance at normal Sunday services remains low; attendance at festival services, such as the excellent flower festival service last night, is high and rising; interest in church affairs is probably greater than at any time since the Norman Conquest.

31 July 1995

The little boy aged nine had a lolly in his mouth when he arrived at the service this morning in Orton Malborne Community Centre in Peterborough. When he had sucked it down to the stick, his mother gave him two more lollies. He put one in his mouth and the other in his pocket. After I had given a little sermon for the children, he went out with the children to Sunday School still sucking the lolly. When he returned half an hour later he was sucking the second lolly. While we adults were sipping coffee after the service the boy came up to me. 'Look, my teeth are falling out.' Sure enough, all his front teeth were missing and the remaining teeth were black.

The people in Orton Malborne are not poor in the way that hundreds of millions of people are poor in Asia and Africa. They have enough food; they have clean water to drink; and when they are sick, there are doctors and hospitals to provide medicines. Yet in India and Africa, the poor whom I have seen seem to have an instinct for survival, while here there is an urge towards self-destruction. This boy is one of five, living in a small flat with their mother; their various fathers have no contact. She gives him lollies to keep him quiet, and probably makes no connection between the lollies and his blackened teeth. Drugs are rife in Orton, so there is every chance that crack will eventually replace sugar as his source of comfort. The green spaces are usually deserted, even on warm summer days, so presumably the children and teenagers spend most of their time indoors watching television or playing computer games. Only at night do the teenagers emerge, and clumps of them can be seen hanging round the alleys or sitting on the benches in the shopping centre. Twenty years ago, when Orton Malborne was being built, I remember wandering round it and admiring its imaginative design. Today it is shabby, with paint peeling from window frames, rusting hulks of cars in the parking spaces, and graffiti daubed on the walls.

A fortnight ago I wrote a letter to the churchwardens of Upton, Hamerton and the five rebel parishes in Breckland, telling them that, now they have broken free from the financial shackles of their dioceses, they must reach out in love to churches in need. If they used this freedom simply to build up financial reserves in the church accounts, or as an excuse to put less in the collection, they would be betraying the gospel. And I proposed that they devote half their weekly collection to supporting youth work in Orton Malborne, enabling the Christian Presence there to employ someone to start youth clubs, drop-in centres and the like.

I used far more forthright language than I would usually dare. The letter was not just a way of raising money, but was a test of their Christian resolve. If they had reacted negatively, giving all sorts of excuses as to why they could not contribute, I would have felt that our entire venture had gone astray. Indeed, I would have been tempted to agree with the bishops, that only if a tax is imposed on the richer churches can money be redistributed to the poorer ones. But within hours of receiving my letter churchwardens from all the parishes telephoned me, saying that they were delighted to have an opportunity to serve their poorer brothers and sisters in some specific way, and they would do just as I suggested. And these churchwardens also began to wonder about organizing special fund-raising events over and above their basic gift.

Not only does this vindicate their rebellion, but it also creates a most unusual, and even prophetic, pattern of ministry in Orton Malborne. In most churches the pastor – the vicar, priest, minister or whatever – receives a salary, while everyone else gives their time freely; this system is so common that no one questions it. In the Christian Presence the pastor, Edie Garvie, is unpaid, but the youth worker will receive a salary. This is far closer to the New Testament. As far as we can tell, the only people deemed worthy of receiving financial support for their ministry were apostles and evangelists, as such work required total commitment of time and energy. Pastors, by contrast, were seen as exercising one ministry amongst many, and so had to support themselves. Our youth worker in Orton Malborne should undoubtedly count as an evangelist. As a Catholic priest said to me recently, waving his hand in the direction of Orton Malborne: 'That is a far tougher mission field than anywhere in Africa.'

What a difference it would make to churches throughout Britain if financial resources and effort were diverted away from pastorship to evangelism – away from just keeping the church going, towards reaching out to the wider community.

6 August 1995

Seven days ago Kit decided that from next month onwards he would begin to conduct worship again in the five rebel parishes, probably on alternate weeks. I doubt if he was ever a robust person, either emotionally or mentally; the events of the past year have badly fractured his self-confidence, leaving him quite terrified of those in positions of authority. So his decision is an act of immense courage. He knows full well that, as a defrocked priest, he risks bringing the entire weight of ecclesiastical wrath on to his head.

But 48 hours after Kit told the churchwardens and me of his intention, the Bishop of Norwich announced that on 27 September he will license a new permanent priest, Graham Drake, to all 10 of Kit's old parishes – both the conformist parishes and the rebels. The archdeacon immediately convened a meeting with the rebel churchwardens, and told them that the bishop had legal powers to impose a priest without their consent, quoting the Benefices Measure of 1986. He claimed that people from the conformist parishes were legally entitled to represent the benefice as a whole in approving the new priest. No sooner had the meeting ended than my answering machine filled with messages from the churchwardens asking my advice.

Despite my unsuitable brain – it operates by intuition rather than logic – I have, over the past two years, become quite an expert in church law. I have purchased all the relevant Acts and Measures from Her Majesty's Stationery Office, and, tutored by David Way, have absorbed their contents. So I was able to pronounce that the archdeacon is wrong. The law to which he refers is clear that every parish must approve a new permanent priest, and can thus veto anyone the bishop proposes. In legal terms the status which the rebels want is a continuous 'interregnum'. And while in the past this would not have been legally possible, a quirk of an earlier law, the Pastoral Measure of 1983, permits it.

But legal details form only a minor sub-plot in this story. The immediate consequence was that Kit telephoned me in some distress to say that his courage was failing him. And Susie telephoned me to pour out her worries about Kit: that if he was caught in some head-to-head conflict with the new priest, with all the attendant publicity, he would break under the strain. I replied that I did not foresee any kind of direct confrontation. Graham Drake, like Tony Foottit at present, would hold token services in the rebel churches, which no local people would attend, and the rebel services would continue, with large congregations. This only partly reassured Kit and Susie. So as a compromise I suggested that Kit could preach every two or three weeks, with someone else leading the prayers; then he would risk less episcopal aggravation. This seemed to calm their nerves.

This morning 50 rebels gathered at Threxton church for the annual Lammas service, when the first corn of the harvest is ceremonially offered to God. Dot had arranged for some wheat from their fields to be ground into flour, and with it she had baked a huge loaf. It was carried up the aisle by two women who were visibly buckling under the weight, and they then dropped it into my arms, leaving me to heave it on to the altar. Afterwards we all drove up the hill for a lavish lunch at Cyril and Dot's rambling farmhouse, where my original meeting with the rebel churchwardens took place last January. Afterwards Kit and I joined the churchwardens on three large oak benches in the garden, to discuss strategy. The churchwardens decided that they will formally announce that Kit and I are 'ministers' in the five parishes – the terms vicar, rector and priest all have awkward legal connotations. They also decided to write to the Bishop of Norwich to tell him that they will not recognize the priest he is appointing, not only on legal grounds, but more importantly on biblical grounds: in the New Testament churches ministry was always with the consent of the people; by specifically refusing to seek the consent of the five rebel parishes, he is contravening Scripture.

No doubt when the new man is installed next month, he will make a concerted effort to defeat the rebels. As far as Sunday worship is concerned, he will have no greater success than the archdeacon: people will simply ignore the services he conducts. The potential weakness for the rebels is public opinion amongst the non-attenders in the villages. The new priest will try to convince them – as the archdeacon has tried – that weddings and funerals organized by the rebel churchwardens are illegal; and people may conclude that it is safer to accept a priest appointed by the bishop than to support the rebels. To counter the possibility, Kit is going to don his dog collar again, and visit as many homes as possible over the next two months.

Over the past six months the churchwardens have become increasingly convinced of the rightness of their rebellion and thence increasingly determined to stand firm. It is a happy accident that the letter of the law is on their side. And since most people like to abide by the law, this might encourage people in other parishes across the country to follow. Yet it is even more likely that the church as a whole will over the next decade catch up with Breckland, Upton and Hamerton. The arrangement which the churchwardens are making with Kit is identical to that which churchwardens in three Suffolk parishes are making with Richard Titford – the difference being that the bishop in Suffolk is in favour of it. And since a direct contract between parishes and their priest conforms to historical tradition and to modern management practice, it will gradually become the norm.

3 September 1995

They clapped their hands and stamped their feet at the hymns I played on my guitar, and they cried out unintelligible words of praise, as in a charismatic prayer meeting. But whether they really understood that we were giving thanks to God for the fruits of the earth, I'm not so sure. At the end they had a good game of rugby with one of these fruits, a large vegetable marrow.

At one end of Orton Malborne is a vast centre for mentally handicapped adults. In fact, it's on the border of Orton Malborne and a rather posh parish filled with mock-Tudor villas built between the wars. Edie has decided that we must make spiritual contact with the mentally handicapped residents, and so organized a harvest festival service; and she got me to conduct it. Throughout the morning I was trembling: I didn't feel frightened of the people themselves, but felt horribly uncertain of my own ability to handle such a situation. Besides I had no idea what kind of service would be appropriate. So I put together a simple hymn-sheet for those who can read, with the usual harvest hymns plus a few simple choruses. And I planned in my mind some activities that might illustrate the theme. But as for an order of service, I reckoned it was best to play it by ear.

The main hall of the centre was packed. Shortly before the service was due to start, the senior therapist explained that they were always short of staff on a Sunday, so they might not be able to keep the place quiet. Her prophecy was fulfilled. The choruses were fine, because if I clapped and stamped in time to the music the patients quickly got the rhythm. 'We plough the fields and scatter' degenerated into a solid roar – like that of a combine harvester at full speed. My activities enjoyed mixed success. A piece I had planned based on television adverts bombed: as the therapist kindly explained afterwards, to most of the residents television is simply an interesting noise in the background, so my allusion to particular products was lost. But imagining ourselves to be seeds sown by Jesus was a hit. We all took our shoes and socks off, and walked round the hall pretending to feel the different sorts of ground beneath our feet – a cold path, sharp stones, thorns and thistles, and soft, moist earth. The theological meaning of all this may have become blurred, but everyone was laughing happily.

Although staff were in short supply, I was amazed at their skill in dealing with the patients. To my shame I found many of the residents physically repulsive; indeed, so strong was my reaction, I felt myself to be a hypocrite in their midst. But the staff exuded genuine love. During the service three residents reacted badly to all the excitement, screaming and crying. In each case a member of staff was able to give immediate comfort, with a perfect mixture of tenderness and firmness. The work of the centre is manifestly the Christian gospel in action; it puts our ecclesiastical squabbles in their proper perspective.

Yet even here the squabbles intruded. I had written to the vicar of the posh parish, asking him to come to the service and speak. He wrote back saying that he could not possibly worship with me, as I was 'fomenting schism' in the church. His words show how deeply rooted the centralizing tendency has become. Unity to most clergy means subservience to the hierarchy – which, as we have been discovering, is how the hierarchy themselves see it. Thus anyone who speaks against the hierarchy, and pleads for greater local autonomy, is seen as 'schismatic'. I fear that this vicar is typical of modern clergy: the old tradition of clerical independence has finally been expunged from the clerical mind, and the clergy now truly see themselves as employees of the bishop. So after 13 centuries the Roman party at the Synod of Whitby has finally proved victorious – at least over the clergy. The question is whether the Celtic fire is being rekindled amongst the laity.

27 September 1995

'He can come in to the church, say a few words to himself, and then go away. We won't try to stop him.' Thus spoke Cyril Lake to the television camera this morning, describing the new priest, Graham Drake, coming to conduct worship at Threxton church.

I too was interviewed. 'It's said that without your leadership the rebellion would not have got this far,' Mike Wooldridge, the BBC's religious affairs correspondent, suggested.

'Not all all,' I replied. 'The leadership comes from these remarkable churchwardens – I simply do what they ask.' The question itself revealed the line which the church authorities are taking: that I am the Rasputin, manipulating innocent lay people in pursuit of my own purposes. It's a clever argument: since my 'crusade' is entirely about handing leadership to the laity, the notion that I am the real leader of the rebels implies simultaneously that I am dishonest, and that the laity are too dumb to provide leadership. The only trouble with this line is that it's wrong; the churchwardens really *are* the leaders.

By seven o'clock this evening Cyril Lake and the other nine churchwardens, plus a large bevy of supporters, were assembled outside Great Cressingham church – one of the conformist churches – where Graham Drake was to be licensed. Susie had made large yellow badges for them all to wear, saying 'Oxborough Circuit', the name which the rebel parishes have given themselves. When the bishop arrived they handed him a letter explaining the moral, spiritual and legal reasons why they could not accept Graham Drake's ministry. The churchwardens and the bishops exchanged no words; the only sound was the whirr of television cameras.

Behind the bishop came about 30 clergy – the bishop had apparently begged them to attend – to show support in front of the cameras. They proved much noisier, loudly accusing the rebels of 'heresy' and 'schism'. Then about 30 lay people appeared; they turned out to be mainly wives of the noisy clergymen. Amidst all this barely a dozen people from the conformist parishes came to welcome their new priest. Afterwards my answering machine filled with messages from happy rebels, convinced that they had won another media victory – which indeed they had.

Why is Graham Drake doing this? Why is he letting himself be used in this way? Does he see himself as conducting a 'crusade' to rid these rebel parishes of heresy and to heal a schism? Or is he simply a loyal servant of the bishop, going where the bishop sends him? To my relief the rebel churchwardens say repeatedly: 'We have nothing against Mr Drake personally; and we wish him a happy ministry in the five conformist parishes. We simply cannot accept his ministry here.' This attitude displays a spiritual maturity which is quite rare in the church: they are disapproving of the action a man is taking, without passing judgment on the man himself. If the Bishop of Norwich had displayed a similar attitude towards Kit and the rebels the problems may have been resolved months ago.

Last Sunday, with trembling limbs, Kit preached his first full-scale sermon since his sacking; it was at the Oxborough Harvest Festival. This Sunday he preaches again at Bodney Harvest Festival. For the first time since I've known him there seems to be fire in his belly, so he actually wants to preach. Until now I think he has seen himself merely as defending his own integrity and good name. But now he is beginning to grasp that the issues at stake go far beyond himself; as he said on the phone tonight, 'I am just a catalyst.' And that makes him feel better.

22 October 1995

The people of Upton and Hamerton had their moment of high drama almost two years ago. I suspect that the high drama in Breckland is almost over. Now we settle down to the long haul. In Upton and Hamerton there has for many months been an air of normality. The conflict with the diocese seems a long time ago, and the people now take it for granted that managing the church and organizing its ministry is their business – and they quietly get on with it. It will be more difficult to feel normal in Breckland because while Graham Drake is still trying to be vicar of the rebel parishes there will be a degree of tension, and at any time things might erupt in a new and unexpected fashion.

In recent weeks the phrase 'Love thine enemies' has kept popping into my head. It is said that this command is unique to Christ; all the rest of his teaching can be found either in the Old Testament or the Greek philosophers. There are two ways in which we can fail to obey it. The first – and obvious – way is to hate our enemies. Perhaps the people of Breckland don't actually hate Bishop Nott, but the contempt in which some of them hold him gets close to it. Perhaps the Bishop of Norwich doesn't actually hate Kit Chalcraft, the parishioners of Breckland and me, but his behaviour hasn't always been gracious. A common enemy certainly helps to bind the Breckland people together and gives an extra zing to our gatherings; if the Bishop of Norwich were to climb down, and Graham Drake were to withdraw, our congregation would probably dwindle. And that would be the moment when the rebellion was really tested. Would there still be a good core of committed people? Would the churchwardens continue to manage affairs with the same degree of care and devotion? I hope – and I expect – the answer would be positive: the churchwardens and the people would be under no illusion that the church and its future depended on them, so complacency would be impossible.

But my point is that the rebellion will only be truly Christian when hatred and contempt have disappeared, and only love remains.

There is another way in which people can disobey Christ's command: they can fail to recognize their enemies for what they are. In fact, this failure is far more common. To admit that we have enemies is to upset our peace of mind, so it's far easier to pretend they don't exist. Over the past half century the men who run the central institutions of the Church (and they are mainly men) have to an extent become enemies of the parishes. They don't intend to be enemies; on the contrary, their motives are good, and they believe themselves to be serving the parishes' interests. And this palpable benevolence makes it doubly difficult for parishes to resist what they are doing. The Bishop of Norwich's behaviour tore the scales from Breckland eyes, so they could see that something in the system is wrong. But Peter Nott in normal circumstances is no doubt decent and honourable, like others who work in the upper echelons. And it is extremely hard for most parishioners in most parishes to regard decent, honourable people as enemies.

It's small wonder that the dictum 'Love thine enemies' is unique to Christ; obeying it requires a psychological somersault. But if the present rebellion is to lead to a spiritual resurrection, all of us must make that somersault. Those of us caught up in Breckland itself must turn hatred into love. Those in parishes elsewhere must acknowledge that good, honest people can also be enemies.

25 October 1995

'If there were a re-match today of the Synod of Whitby, the Celts would certainly beat the Romans.' That hypothetical prediction was made in May by a member of the audience at Southwell Minster in Nottinghamshire. I had been asked to speak on 'Celtic Christianity, Past and Present'. The canon organizing the event had put out 40 seats in the nave. In fact, so popular is the subject that over 200 people came, causing the canon and vergers – and I – to scurry round dragging piles of plastic chairs from side chapels into the nave. Certainly in that group there was no doubt where sympathies lay when I described the Synod.

And I think that member of the audience is right about public opinion generally. Thirteen centuries ago Wilfred's disparaging remarks about Celtic narrow-mindedness carried weight amongst kings and chieftains who admired the more sophisticated culture of continental Europe. But while Celtic Christianity may have been insular in its art and literature, it was wonderfully open and broad in its attitude to faith and morality. It offered to people direct spiritual experience, instead of dry doctrines handed down by theologians; and it stressed compassion and love for all creatures over and above compliance with ethical rules. Today, people seek artistic and literary stimulus from secular sources, so Wilfred's arguments find no echo. When they turn to religion, the great majority want just what Celtic Christianity can give.

The trouble is that as yet very few churches are Celtic: the descendants of Wilfred still hold the reins of ecclesiastical power and dominate Christian thought. As a result, I fear that fewer and fewer people look to the church, or to Jesus Christ himself, to satisfy their spiritual needs. Go into any bookshop and you find huge numbers of books on spiritual matters, usually on shelves marked 'Mind, Body, Spirit' but the number of Christian books is minuscule – and, according to my publishing friends, continuing to fall.

Paradoxically, the better books in the 'Mind, Body, Spirit' section share many insights with the great Celtic saints and seers, but these insights are rarely to be found in Christian books, which are mostly still infused with the spirit of Wilfred.

Yet, as the popularity of the Celtic event in Southwell Minster demonstrated, the Celtic wind is beginning to blow once again through the churches. Indeed, I spoke last year at a similar event held outdoors in Bradwell in Essex, where the Celtic saint Cedd had his base; and over 1,500 people turned up. And even where Christians do not identify their ideas as Celtic, the kind of thinking which would have been familiar to Columba, Aidan and Cuthbert is increasingly to be found in our pews. The people of Upton, Hamerton and Breckland were largely ignorant of the Celtic tradition when they began to mount their rebellion. But when I spoke about Celtic Christianity, they were delighted; and in Breckland, Fursey, the Irish monk who landed near Yarmouth and evangelized Norfolk, has become their patron saint.

I don't for one minute expect that these rebellions in remote East Anglian villages will trigger any kind of wider revolt across the country. That is not how change normally occurs. But I do regard them as signs of the times. And as such they are giving a jolt to Christianity in a Celtic direction. I believe that Christianity in Britain must either go much further in that direction over the next three or four decades, or risk extinction. Christianity has virtually died out in many of the countries where it once flourished, and there is no guarantee that the same will not happen here. The Celtic vision offers hope.

Upton, Hamerton, Threxton, Oxborough, Little Cressingham, Didlington, Bodney, Orton Malborne and Richard Titford's parishes of Little Waldingfield, Edwardstone and Groton – these are all places where the Synod of Whitby is being replayed in miniature. It will be through lots of local matches, mostly played without fuss or publicity, that the gospel preached by Columba, Aidan, Cuthbert and Fursey will be heard again in our land.

POSTSCRIPT

Opting Out – A Practical Guide for Parishes

Most church people are deeply conservative by temperament, wanting to uphold and even restore traditions; and they also wish to abide by the law. As the stories related in this book illustrate, the current centralization of finance and management in the Church of England is a historical aberration; the English – indeed the British – tradition is for local churches to enjoy a high degree of autonomy. And as the experience of the parishes described in this book reveals, recent changes in church law can be used to reassert this autonomy. Every parish which decides to opt out of central control will strengthen the case for this course of action, showing to bishops, clergy and laity alike that it makes both practical and spiritual sense. So I happily offer a step-by-step guide to opting out.

1. Decide What Pattern of Ministry You Want and Can Afford

The cost of a full-time vicar is his/her salary plus working expenses. There is no guarantee that an opt-out parish would be permitted to use the vicarage; this would be a matter of negotiation with the diocese and the Church Commissioners. So the vicar's salary would perhaps have to be large enough to cover the cost of living accommodation. There are many parishes or groups of parishes which can afford a full-time vicar, and want one. But other patterns of ministry can be equally, or even more, effective, and much cheaper. There may be retired or 'non-stipendiary' clergy living in the area who can be invited to conduct services. More importantly, congregations should look to the spiritual gifts amongst themselves. There will be some who are good at visiting the sick and welcoming newcomers; some who are good at arranging special festival services; and some who can conduct worship well, and even preach. Thus a congregation may be able to organize its own non-sacramental services. And it may put forward one or two of its members to train for the ordained ministry.

2. Appoint Good 'Managers' of the Parish

The key to opting out is that the parish, or group of parishes, must be able to manage its own affairs competently. Traditionally, the churchwardens have been the parish managers; so a parish or group considering this course should ensure that people with managerial ability occupy this office. One of the churchwardens should then become chairman of the Parochial Church Council or Group Council; this person is thus in a position to provide the necessary impetus and leadership.

3. Consult the Vicar

Much depends on the needs and feelings of the present vicar. If he is about to retire or move to a new post, that obviously leaves the parish free to determine its own future. Yet even if the vicar wishes to stay, he or she may welcome the idea of being paid directly by the parish, and hence be more clearly accountable to the people. Since all clergy are technically self-employed there is no legal impediment against making this change. Equally, some clergy may wish to work only part-time, receiving only half a salary, and make up the rest of their income by other means; there are much greater opportunities for this flexible style of working today than in the past. And clergy approaching retirement age may be especially pleased at the possibility of remaining within the parish and continuing to conduct services and visiting people on a voluntary basis, but being free of administrative chores.

4. Consult the Parishioners

There is a widespread notion that being part of the financial and administrative structures of the diocese somehow guarantees that a church will remain open and have a vicar. In fact, the opposite is the case. Dioceses have never provided money to maintain church buildings; this is entirely the responsibility of the parishioners, and the various state and charitable agencies which offer help.

Equally, most dioceses have now made clear that, when parishes do not pay enough money through the quota to finance their clergy, the clergy will be withdrawn. So the only guarantee lies with the parishioners themselves. It is probably worthwhile to convene an open meeting to explain this and thus to show that opting out offers the best prospect for long-term survival. Once people – even those who rarely attend worship – understand that the future of their parish church depends on them, they will be far more ready to contribute in both time and money. It may also be important to reassure people that baptisms, weddings and funerals will still take place.

5. Determine a Strategy and Time-scale

The churchwardens and council members must now draw all the threads together with a precise plan. This plan should include:

- the type of services to be held, their frequency, and the people conducting them
- pastoral care, especially of the elderly and the sick, and the welcoming of newcomers
- financial budgets for the next five years or so.

In making this plan, it will become clear when the parish should actually take the plunge.

6. Consult the Authorities

If there is reason to believe that the bishop and/or archdeacon may be sympathetic, it is appropriate to discuss matters at an earlier stage. But if they are likely to be hostile, or at best discouraging, then it is wiser to wait until the plan is fully formulated. At this point a letter should be sent to the bishop informing him of the parish's intentions. In any meetings which may ensue, it is important to remember that, while the bishop has an important spiritual role, his actual powers – both in law and according to tradition – are quite limited. Since the bishop may want to assert more power than he actually possesses, it is important to be conversant with the law.

7. *Know the Law – Pastoral Measure 1983*

This statute allows a bishop, after consulting the PCC, to 'suspend the presentation' to a parish. Historically, the patron of a parish, who was usually a local person, 'presented' a clergyman to a parish, often after consulting local feelings, and that clergyman was then formally inducted to the parish by the bishop. The clergyman became known as rector or vicar, and enjoyed the 'freehold' of the parish. He enjoyed a high degree of independence, so the bishop could not interfere in parish affairs. 'Suspending the presentation' means that, for a period, this process does not apply. Instead, after consulting the PCC, the bishop can appoint a temporary 'priest-in-charge'.

The purpose of this provision was to give bishops a degree of flexibility when parishes were being rearranged; it was envisaged that the presentation would be suspended for a few years at most. In practice bishops have suspended presentation in countless parishes, renewing the suspension every five years, and in this way have greatly extended their powers to deploy clergy, and to hire and fire them, as they wish.

However, this can be turned to the advantage of parishes who wish to organize their own pastoral ministry. In legal terms a parish where the presentation has been suspended is in indefinite interregnum – and this is precisely what an opting-out parish wants. In this situation the churchwardens and PCC have full powers to invite people to conduct services as they wish, making whatever financial arrangements they deem appropriate, and to organize visiting of the sick and elderly.

So if the bishops can get away with increasing their powers by suspending presentations indefinitely, the laity can do the same.

8. *Know the Law – Patronage (Benefices) Measure 1986*

This statute had the admirable intention of giving churchwardens and PCCs far greater influence in the choice of their priest. When a priest leaves, the PCC is invited to prepare 'a statement describing the conditions, needs and traditions of the parish', and to appoint 'two lay members of the council to act as lay representatives in connection with the selection of an incumbent'. These two people are often the churchwardens. These lay representatives meet any prospective incumbent, and a person can only be appointed with their approval.

If a parish wishes to make its own pastoral arrangements, it can simply refuse to approve anyone who is proposed as incumbent. In honesty, it should state in advance that this is its intention; thus its refusal implies no personal dislike of any prospective priest. The statute seems to suggest that the lay representatives can continue to withhold approval indefinitely.

There is, however, some doubt as to the meaning of the word 'incumbent'. Strictly speaking, the word refers only to a rector or vicar. But authoritative commentaries, such as the current edition of Sir William Dale's classic book (*The Law of the Parish Church*, Butterworth, 1989), make clear that the word also applies to a permanent priest-in-charge. And since 1986 all dioceses have followed this procedure in appointing parish clergy, regardless of whether they are rectors, vicars or priests-in-charge.

9. Set the Law Aside

The law is only invoked when there is a dispute. Parishes wanting to 'opt-out' should try to obtain either the agreement of the bishop, or at least his tacit acceptance. If a parish or group decides to keep its present clergyman, but to pay him or her directly, the parish or group is entirely free to do this – there is no legal impediment. The same applies if the clergyman becomes half-time or decides to take no salary at all. Equally, there is no logical or legal reason why a bishop should not allow a parish to enter an indefinite interregnum, in which it invites clergymen to conduct the sacramental services. Indeed, some bishops appear to be actively encouraging this, and urging men and women in such parishes to offer themselves for the non-stipendiary ministry. There is every hope that over the next few years an increasing number of bishops will allow and even help parishes to 'opt out'; parishes wanting to do this should make every effort to persuade their bishop of its virtues.

10. Consider the Quota

Contrary to what many believe, the quota – the annual sum which dioceses request from parishes – is a purely voluntary payment. Dioceses are increasingly resorting to a form of coercion to secure payment, by implying – or in some cases clearly stating – that they will no longer supply a priest to parishes which default. The parishes should properly turn this threat back on the dioceses, by responding that they no longer want a priest supplied to them, but will make their own arrangements. As every PCC member knows, the quota has been rising steeply in recent years, owing partly to the reckless depletion of Church Commissioners' assets, and will continue to rise for some years to come. As a result many parishes simply cannot afford to remain inside the centralized financial system; they must opt out or die. A parish which opts out should stop paying its quota, since the diocese is no longer paying the salary of its clergy. Nonetheless, it may consider making some contribution towards the central costs of the diocese. The best way of calculating a fair contribution is to obtain a copy of the diocesan accounts, and tick off those costs which are worthwhile; these may include such items as mission, youth work and so on. The parish can then work out very approximately its fair share of these costs.

11. Pray

Opting out may be a means of resolving financial problems, and the law may be used as a tool to enable it to happen. But first and foremost it is a spiritual and pastoral step, aimed at restoring our traditional pattern of ministry and mutual care. So it will only work well if at every stage it is guided and sustained by prayer.

By Sex Divided
The Church of England and Women Priests

Jonathan Petre

By the summer of 1994, more than 1200 women had been ordained as priests in the Church of England. Few issues have provoked such rancour and bitterness, division and dissent. *By Sex Divided* captures some of the flavour of these extraordinary times – from the early struggles of women to make their voices heard to the dramatic denouement on November 11 1993, and its aftermath.

Jonathan Petre, a journalist who covered much of the debate, calls on the observations of some of the leading protagonists including Dr Robert Runcie, Dr George Carey, Dr Graham Leonard, Peter Geldard, George Austin, Diana McClatchey and Joyce Bennett.

The Archbishop of Canterbury, Dr George Carey, is now involved in a damage-limitation exercise attempting to reconcile the opposing views and to accommodate those who feel uneasy about women priests within the Church. Petre examines the effects of this issue and the future now facing the Church of England.

'If anyone wants to know how it really felt to be there, and how the Church arrived at where it is now, the most graphic and accurate account so far is in *By Sex Divided* . . .'

Church Times

'As a blow-by-blow account of one particular, and very significant, high-profile campaign it is hard to imagine the book being bettered.'

Daily Telegraph

Children of Chernobyl

The human cost of the world's worst nuclear disaster

Adi Roche

Adi Roche's involvement with Chernobyl led right into the 'purple zone' itself, which on 26 April 1986 became the most radioactive place on earth. The radioactivity was ninety times the level of the Hiroshima bomb and will remain harmful for at least a thousand years. 170,000 children under seven received doses high enough to cause thyroid cancer.

In 1991 the Irish Campaign for Nuclear Disarmament (ICND) and the Cork Youth Association responded to a call by American and Belorussian doctors to receive 60 children from Chernobyl for rest and healing in Ireland. The Chernobyl Children's Project was formed in association with ICND and soon Adi Roche, the Project workers and volunteers began to organize convoys to the contaminated areas of Belarus, the country which received over 70 per cent of the radioactive fallout. These convoys brought urgently needed medical aid.

Children of Chernobyl is the vivid and shocking account of the 1986 disaster and its aftermath. Although its conclusions are depressing and contrast strongly with the claims of the nuclear industry, the book also records the efforts of individuals offering hope to live and the hand of friendship to the embattled people of Belarus, Western Russia and the Ukraine.

Adi Roche has recently been awarded the prestigious title Irish European of the Year 1996. All royalties from the sale of this book will go to the Chernobyl Children's Project.

Set My People Free

An Appeal to the Churches

Ruth Etchells

The Archbishop of Canterbury's Lent Book 1996

Ruth Etchells' dynamic new book describes the crucial difference between the Church of God and its outward and visible form, the institutional Church. We must never forget that the Church we know exists only to serve God's wider purposes in the world. When it becomes an end in itself, it has failed.

The work of the Church has never been so urgently required. Not only must it bring together the community of Christians in worship, but also let the world know that it stands against many of the values to which modern society adheres – above all, self-interest.

Most significantly, this book proposes that it is the laity who are the 'secret army' of God. They live out in the world and are best equipped to confront it, yet they seem only to support the work of the clergy, making no real contribution themselves. They must be set free to serve God in their own way, in all the richness of the living faith.

Celtic Journeys
in Scotland and the North of England

Shirley Toulson

As interest grows in Britain's Celtic heritage, Shirley Toulson's book provides an easy guide to the places associated with its remarkable teachers and missionaries – the Celtic Saints.

Celtic Journeys contains eight tours, each based upon the movements of specific individuals and their followers. They include Ninian, Kentigern, Columba, Kenneth, Adomnan, Cuthbert, Aidan and Hilda.

With informative maps to accompany the tours, this beautiful book will help the traveller to understand the way in which the Celtic Saints turned their backs on the dark centuries that preceded their emergence, bringing the light of learning and of faith to the barbarous tribes of England and Scotland.

Dead Man Walking

Helen Prejean

Now a major motion picture, starring Susan Sarandon and Sean Penn; directed by Tim Robbins.

When Sr Helen Prejean is invited to write to a prisoner on Death Row who brutally killed two teenagers, she has little idea how much it will change her life. Although she abhors his crime, she befriends one man as he faces the electric chair.

Dead Man Walking is Helen Prejean's gripping true story, which forms the basis for one of the major cinema events of the year. As powerful an indictment of the death penalty as has ever been written, her book was nominated for the Pulitzer Prize.

'Susan Sarandon gives the finest performance of her career.'
Cosmopolitan

'Though Sarandon and Penn would be strong enough to carry a two-character movie, "Walking" is much, much more. It's fabulous.'
New York Times

'An extraordinary, compelling account of involvement with death row prisoners.'
The Independent

'The most moving memoir of relationships with condemned men since Capote's "In Cold Blood".'
The New Yorker

The Gospel According to Woman

Karen Armstrong

The Gospel According to Woman provides a passionate and provocative interpretation of the history of women in Christianity – a history blighted by the neuroses of a patriarchal Western culture.

Although early Christianity offered a positive message to women, Armstrong argues, by the second century things were taking a distinct turn for the worst. In succeeding ages, the combined effects of Western scholasticism and theology have forced women into certain stereotypical roles – the virgin, martyr, witch, wife and mother.

The message is not wholly negative, and Armstrong shows how many women have shrugged off these stereotypes. In fact, our Christian heritage has had much to do with the redressing of the sexual balance in recent years, and continues to add positive and creative elements to our culture. Rigorously researched and well-informed, this book is a brilliant polemical *tour de force* by the author of *A History of God*.